SpringerBriefs in Computer Science

More information about this series at http://www.springer.com/series/10028

Oge Marques

Innovative Technologies in Everyday Life

 Springer

Oge Marques
Department of Computer and Electrical
    Engineering and Computer Science
Florida Atlantic University
Boca Raton, FL, USA

ISSN 2191-5768   ISSN 2191-5776   (electronic)
SpringerBriefs in Computer Science
ISBN 978-3-319-45697-3   ISBN 978-3-319-45699-7   (eBook)
DOI 10.1007/978-3-319-45699-7

Library of Congress Control Number: 2016951455

Printed on acid-free paper

This Springer imprint is published by Springer Nature
The registered company is Springer International Publishing AG
The registered company address is Gewerbestrasse 11, 6330 Cham, Switzerland

To Ingrid

Preface

This short book provides an overview of contemporary innovative technologies and discusses their impact on our daily lives. Written from a technical perspective, and yet using language and terminology accessible to nonexperts, it describes the technologies, the key players in each area, and the most popular apps and services (and their pros and cons), as well as relevant usage statistics.

It is targeted at a broad audience, ranging from young gadget enthusiasts to senior citizens trying to get used to new devices and associated apps. By offering a structured overview of some of the most useful technologies currently available, putting them in perspective, and suggesting numerous resources for further exploration, the book gives its readers a clear path for learning new topics through apps and Web based resources, making better choices of apps and websites for frequent use, using social networks effectively, protecting their privacy and staying safe online, and enjoying the opportunities brought about by these technological advances without being completely consumed by them.

I expect that the book will fulfill its goal of serving as a preliminary reference on the subject. Readers who want to deepen their understanding of specific topics will find more than two hundred references to additional sources of related information.

I want to express my gratitude to Dr. Herb Shapiro—Associate Provost and Director of the Lifelong Learning Society (LLS) at Florida Atlantic University (FAU), Boca Raton, FL—and the LLS patrons, board, and staff for their encouragement and support during the occasions in which I had the pleasure of teaching topics related to this book to groups of intellectually curious lifelong learners.

I would also like to thank Courtney Dramis, Jennifer Malat, Jennifer Evans, and their team at Springer for their support throughout this project.

Boca Raton, FL, USA   Oge Marques
June 2016

Contents

Chapter 1
Introduction

Abstract Mobile apps, smartphones, and social networks have forever changed the way we go about our everyday activities, such as reading the news, getting traffic directions to our next destination, watching TV, taking pictures, or staying in touch with friends and family. This book offers an easy-to-read introduction to selected new technologies and provides many practical tips on how to best use them.

1.1 Motivation

We live in a world connected by social networks and dominated by technological advances that include a myriad of apps and gadgets, such as tablets and smartphones. Facebook, Twitter, iPhone, iPad, Skype, YouTube, Netflix, Amazon, and Instagram (to mention but a few) have become household names. This has created a true revolution in many fields of human activity, including how we read the news, get traffic directions to our next destination, watch TV, take pictures, check the weather forecast, or update our status and whereabouts for our friends and family members. Together with advances in high-speed cellular data networks and increasing availability of Wi-Fi "hot spots", it has never been easier to stay connected 24/7.

Navigating through this ocean of new technologies and apps (while not losing our minds in the process!) can be challenging. There are too many new things to learn each day! And the goal of mastering a minimally required set of technologies to be considered a "digitally literate" individual is a fast-moving target, which compounds the challenge even further.

This book was written to help readers who want to make sense of some of the most relevant technological advances that are shaping the way we live. It provides an easy-to-read introduction to selected new technologies and discusses how they have grown to become an integral part of our daily lives.

Using language and terminology accessible to non-experts, we will discuss the technologies (and what makes them successful), including relevant historical aspects, essential statistics, the key players in each area, the most popular apps and services, and their pros and cons. Along the way, we will provide many practical

© The Author(s) 2016
O. Marques, *Innovative Technologies in Everyday Life*, SpringerBriefs
in Computer Science, DOI 10.1007/978-3-319-45699-7_1

tips on how to best use these technologies, and suggest ways by which we can put these amazing technological advances to our advantage, rather than being consumed by them.

1.2 Outline of the Book

These are some of the highlights of what we will discuss in the remainder of the book:

- In Chap. 2, we examine how *the Word Wide Web (WWW)* has become an integral part of our lives and has revolutionized just about everything we do. After presenting a historical overview of the evolution of the Web, we explain important concepts and terminology (such as: client, server, browser, HTTP, and HTML), discuss the transition from consumers (Web 1.0) to producers (Web 2.0) of Web-available content, offer suggestions to use Web-based resources for lifelong learning, and offer practical recommendations on matters such as choosing a browser, testing your Internet connection speed, and staying safe online.
- Chapter 3 focuses on *smartphones*. We look at the evolution of telephone communications and the pervasiveness of cellphones, discuss what makes a cellphone a smartphone, and examine key statistics on smartphone usage patterns. We also offer practical advice on which smartphone to purchase, which apps to download, and how to adjust basic the device's privacy and security settings.
- In Chap. 4 we examine *social networks* and their users. After presenting essential statistics from recent studies, we focus on the most popular social networks and discuss their history, jargon, usage, and impact. The chapter contains many practical recommendations for sharing contents on social networks and following the proper etiquette.
- Chapter 5 focuses on apps, gadgets, websites, and social networks whose primary emphasis is on *visual information*. We present a selected set of apps and techniques used to capture, produce, edit, share, remix, and distribute images and videos. We also discuss some of the technical challenges behind the tasks of organizing, annotating, and finding relevant images and videos. Moreover, we analyze changes in TV watching habits and the YouTube phenomenon.
- Finally, Chap. 6 offers some reflections on how these technologies are changing our habits and what the future may hold.

Chapter 2
The World Wide Web

Abstract The Web has become an integral part of our lives and has revolutionized just about everything we do. In this chapter we present a brief historical overview of the evolution of the Web. After introducing important concepts and terminology, we discuss how we have transitioned from being consumers to also becoming producers of Web available content. We postulate that the Web provides a very rich platform for lifelong learning and offer suggestions of sites that can be used for that purpose. The chapter concludes with practical recommendations on browsers, browser extensions, Internet connection speed tests, and staying safe online.

2.1 Introduction

The Word Wide Web (WWW) has become an integral part of our lives and has impacted just about everything we do. Reading the news, checking the weather, purchasing gifts, consulting movie showtimes at the closest theater, applying for a job, looking for new recipes, paying bills, learning new skills, and much, much more can be done entirely over the Web, with great convenience and substantial savings in time, fuel, and paper.

We all use websites and Web-based apps and services on a regular basis, but we may not know what *exactly* is the World Wide Web and what makes it work the way it does. In this chapter you will learn more about the Web, its underlying technologies, historical evolution, and future trends.

To get us started, let's answer a fundamental question: "What, exactly, is the World Wide Web?" According to the Merrian-Webster dictionary, the World Wide Web (or simply *Web*) is "a part of the Internet accessed through a graphical user interface and containing documents often connected by hyperlinks" [3]. The key aspects of this definition are:

- The Web is *a part of* the Internet. The latter is a the worldwide collection of interconnected computer networks, which has existed (since its beginnings as a US Department of Defense computer network known as ARPANET) for decades before the Web was conceived and implemented.
- Web browsers provide access to the content stored in numerous servers around the world through a *graphical user interface* (GUI). One of the major reasons

© The Author(s) 2016

O. Marques, *Innovative Technologies in Everyday Life*, SpringerBriefs in Computer Science, DOI 10.1007/978-3-319-45699-7_2

for the Web's success resides in its interactive and multimedia aspects: images, videos, audio, games, interactive polls, and much more!

- The Web was originally conceived to connect *documents*, but eventually evolved to become a platform for software development. Parallel to this development, Web pages (and sites) gave rise to Web-based *apps* and the Web became a global marketplace for online shopping (also known as *e-commerce*).

A more technical definition could describe the World Wide Web as "a collection of *documents*, with unique names (*addresses* or *URLs*), stored in specialized computers (*servers*), accessible through *browsers*, and interconnected through *hyperlinks*."

A common mistake is to confuse the Web with the Internet at large, Google, your browser, or any specific computer or site. It is none of these things.

2.2   Important Concepts

In this section we present the most important technical terms and acronyms associated with the way the World Wide Web (and the Internet, at large) operate.

Client

A computer that accesses (and interacts with) Web-based content.

Server

A computer that stores Web pages and serves the content to a client upon request.

Website (or simply *site*)

A collection of pages and other assets (images, audio and video files, etc.) that belong together and are accessible over the Web.

Browser

A software program that allows accessing and displaying the contents of Web sites. Examples: Google Chrome, Safari, Mozilla Firefox, Opera, Microsoft Edge, and Internet Explorer.

Browser extension (or *add-on*)

A computer program that extends the functionality of a Web browser in some way.

Search engine

A computer program, usually available as a website, which is used to look for information on the Internet. Examples: Google, Bing, and DuckDuckGo.

Protocol

A set of rules governing the exchange or transmission of data between devices.

HTTP (HyperText Transfer Protocol)

The protocol that establishes how data is exchanged between a server and a client on the Web.

HTML (HyperText Markup Language)

A standardized system for tagging text files to achieve font, color, graphic, and hyperlink effects on Web pages. The latest version is HTML 5.

JavaScript

A computer programming language commonly used to create interactive effects within Web pages.

Flash

A platform for producing and displaying animation and video in Web pages.

ISP (Internet Service Provider)

An organization that provides services for accessing, using, or participating in the Internet. Examples: AOL, AT&T, and Comcast.

Domain name

A unique name that identifies an Internet resource such as a website. Examples: fau.edu, yahoo.com, whitehouse.gov, darpa.mil.

2.3   Milestones in the History of the Web

The history of the Web begins around 1989, when—in a technical report titled "Information Management: A Proposal" [1]—Tim Berners-Lee (then at the European Organization for Nuclear Research (CERN) in Switzerland) produced the earliest design specifications for a global hypertext system. According to Berners-Lee, the document was "an attempt to persuade CERN management that such a system was in the organization's best interests" [1]. Figure 2.1 shows a graphical overview of the proposed system and how it would link documents (and the people who produced them) to other documents (and people), regardless of their physical location. The proposed system was originally called "Mesh"; in 1990, Berners-Lee decided to rename it to "World Wide Web".

During the past 25 years or so, the Web has experienced incredible growth, to the point where we can hardly think of life without it. It has also changed significantly as new browsers, companies, and applications have become available over the years. To give us a sense of perspective on how young some of the Web-based sites and apps that we take for granted actually are and how much has happened during this quarter of century, Table 2.1 summarizes some of the milestones and trends in the history of the Web (see [4] for more).

2.4   Web 2.0: The Shift from Consumer to Producer

One of the most impacting changes in the history of the Web started to happen in the early 2000s: users began to produce content, whereas until that point in time they were primarily consumers of content prepared and posted online by "institutions" (companies, newspapers, universities, etc.). This shift is often referred to as the transition between Web 1.0 to *Web 2.0*, a term popularized by Tim O'Reilly and Dale Dougherty in 2004.

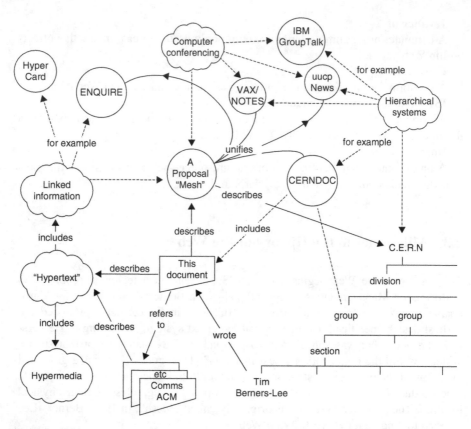

Fig. 2.1 First schematic diagram showing the structure of a proposed "mesh" of hyperlinked documents—which would later become the "World Wide Web" [1]

But what, exactly, makes us producers of content? Every time we *like* a Facebook post, rate a restaurant on Yelp, review a hotel on TripAdvisor or a book on Amazon, upload a picture to Flickr, etc. we become a producer. But to be a true content creator you would need to have a site or, at least, a Tumblr, a personal blog, or Twitter account.

The combination of blog posts, wikis, product reviews, social networks updates, hashtags, tweets, viral videos on YouTube, citizen journalism videos and photos, and a myriad of content production methods has resulted in a type of "collective intelligence" that we have used to rely upon quite frequently.

Table 2.1 Selected milestones in the history of the World Wide Web

Year	Event	Description
1989	Beginnings	Tim Berners-Lee publishes a technical report [1] outlining a system of linked documents which would eventually become the World Wide Web
1989	World's first website	The first website appeared (Fig. 2.2)[a]. It consisted of text (no images!) and included links to several other documents
1993	First browser	Mosaic, the world's first Web browser—originally developed at the at the National Center for Supercomputing Applications (NCSA) at the University of Illinois Urbana-Champaign—is released
1993	Mainstream media attention	The New York Times publishes an article in which Mosaic is described as a "killer app", which they saw as "an applications program so different and so obviously useful that it can create a new industry from scratch" [2]
1994	White House	The White House establishes its official website
1994	Yahoo!	Yahoo! is founded (by Jerry Yang and David Filo) in Sunnyvale, CA. It was originally a hierarchical directory to the contents of the Web at that time, as suggested by its "backronym" (Yet Another Hierarchically Organized Oracle)
1994	First online purchases	Pizza Hut tests PizzaNet, an "electronic storefront" that allowed ordering pizzas online for home delivery in Santa Cruz, CA (Fig. 2.3)
1995	Amazon.com	Amazon.com opens for business, selling books online, offering "one million titles, consistently low prices"
1995	Internet Explorer	Microsoft releases the first version of its browser, to compete against the market leader, Netscape
1997	Google	Google.com is registered as a domain. The name—a play on the word "googol," a mathematical term for the number represented by the numeral 1 followed by 100 zeros—reflects their founders' mission to organize a seemingly infinite amount of information on the Web
2001	Wikipedia	Jimmy Wales launches Wikipedia. Users write over 20,000 encyclopedia entries in the first year alone
2003	Music, blogs, and social networks	The iTunes Music Store is born, revolutionizing the business of online music downloads. During the same year, MySpace, Blogger, WordPress, and LinkedIn make their debut
2004	Facebook	[the] Facebook opens for Harvard students
2004	Firefox	Mozilla launches v. 1.0 of the Firefox Web browser
2005	YouTube	YouTube is founded. Less than 18 months later, it would be acquired by Google for $1.65 billion
2006	Twitter	Twitter—defined then as a "micro-blogging" platform—launches
2008	Chrome	Google releases the Chrome Web browser
2008	HTML5	The latest version of the HTML standard, HTML5, is introduced

(continued)

Table 2.1 (continued)

Year	Event	Description
2008	Deals and coupons	Groupon launches, offering daily deals at restaurants, retailers and service providers
2009	Bing	Microsoft's Bing search engine launches
2010	Photo sharing	Social photo-sharing sites Pinterest and Instagram launch
2010	Quora	Ex-Facebook employees launch user-based question and answer site Quora
2011	Social networks	Google launches an interest-based social network, called Google+
2013	Smartphones and the mobile Web	A majority (56 %) of Americans now own a smartphone of some kind
2014	WhatsApp	Facebook buys messaging app WhatsApp for $19 billion. Less than 2 years later WhatsApp would reach the one billion users milestone

[a]If you are curious about how a page/site used to look like at some point in time, check the *Internet Archive: wayback machine*: http://archive.org/web/

World Wide Web

The WorldWideWeb (W3) is a wide-area hypermedia information retrieval initiative aiming to give universal access to a large universe of documents.

Everything there is online about W3 is linked directly or indirectly to this document, including an executive summary of the project, Mailing lists , Policy , November's W3 news , Frequently Asked Questions .

What's out there?
    Pointers to the world's online information, subjects , W3 servers, etc.
Help
    on the browser you are using
Software Products
    A list of W3 project components and their current state. (e.g. Line Mode ,X11 Viola , NeXTStep , Servers , Tools , Mail robot , Library)
Technical
    Details of protocols, formats, program internals etc
Bibliography
    Paper documentation on W3 and references.
People
    A list of some people involved in the project.
History
    A summary of the history of the project.
How can I help ?
    If you would like to support the web..
Getting code
    Getting the code by anonymous FTP , etc.

Fig. 2.2 The world's first website (currently available at http://info.cern.ch/hypertext/WWW/TheProject.html)

Fig. 2.3 PizzaNet: early example of online shopping (currently available at http://www.pizzahut.
com/assets/pizzanet/home.html)

2.5   New and Better Ways to Learn: A Curated List of Web-Based Resources for Lifelong Learners

The Web is a vast source of information, much of which is free and easily accessible, which can be used to learn just about anything. It is, however, an unwieldily large and rather unstructured source of information which is not often curated or edited properly, leading to two potential problems: (1) information overload; and (2) difficulty selecting reliable contents and sources, rather than noisy ones.

   In this section, I provide recommendations on how to use Google, Wikipedia, Twitter, Facebook and YouTube for casual learning purposes. I also suggest several sites for learning a variety of topics in a more structured way.

2.5.1   Informal Learning

You can use Wikipedia, Twitter, Facebook, YouTube, and several Google products and sites for what I refer to as *informal* or *unstructured* learning. Here are some practical recommendations on how to best use those resources:

Wikipedia

Wikipedia is a free-access, free-content Internet encyclopedia, whose contents are edited by users themselves. It has recently celebrated its 15th anniversary, boasting more than five million articles in its English edition (one of 291 Wikipedia editions available) and becoming the Web's largest and most popular general reference work [5].

I recommend using Wikipedia as a quick-reference source for *preliminary* reading on *noncontroversial* topics. When reading a Wikipedia entry, be mindful that some entries will display warnings that indicate that the page has issues (for example: vague language, lack of external references, biased arguments, etc.). If you need more authoritative sources (e.g., peer-reviewed scholarly journal articles), follow the references to external (reputable) sources usually found at the end of a Wikipedia entry.

Facebook

Facebook can be an excellent source of useful news and information from which we can learn about a wide variety of topics. I recommend that you use Facebook to do one or more of the following: (1) *subscribe* to inspiring feeds; (2) *like* the Facebook pages of people, companies, news sources, you admire; and (3) *follow* the public updates of individual users who are not close enough to be invited to be your friends. To help you get started, these are three of my personal favorites (out of more than 2000):

- Brain Pickings[1]: rich collection of inspiring cross-disciplinary posts on literature, psychology, art, science, design, history, philosophy, and more, curated by writer Maria Popova, an MIT Futures of Entertainment Fellow.
- Harvard Business Review (HBR)[2]: articles and blog posts on management aspects of professional life from Harvard's flagship magazine.
- The British Museum[3]: highlights of the museum's vast collection, explained and contextualized in short and frequent posts.

Twitter

Twitter can be a wonderful source of fresh, relevant information from reputable sources. In Twitter—perhaps more than in any other social media platform—the decision to follow people is based on the quality of what they post. In addition to

---

[1]http://www.facebook.com/brainpickings.mariapopova.
[2]http://www.facebook.com/HBR/.
[3]http://www.facebook.com/britishmuseum.

following people (or institutions) whose updates are of high quality and relevance, you can also "bookmark" your favorite tweets for easy future reference to a particularly informative post.

These are some of my personal favorites to follow on Twitter:

- Engadget[4] (on Twitter: @engadget): Engadget describes itself as "the definitive guide to this connected life". It provides an excellent coverage of devices, gadgets, and technology and occasional discussions on how they impact our lives.
- Bill Gates[5] (on Twitter: @BillGates): Posts from the personal blog of technologist, business leader, and philanthropist Bill Gates where he shares insights and recommendations on books and other ways of learning.
- TED Talks[6] (on Twitter: @TEDTalks): TED contains a vast and rich set of short talks in a broad variety of topics, whose main goal is to spread ideas worth sharing.

YouTube

Video plays a significant role in improving the effectiveness of learning in a variety of ways. Properly produced videos can shed light on difficult subjects, for instance, by using animation to illustrate scientific concepts. Recorded video lectures by world-renowned authorities in their fields of expertise allow us a chance to learn directly from the expert in ways that would not be feasible otherwise. Moreover, video is often the preferred medium for the 'how-to' category, which taps onto skills that are better learned through video, such as playing a musical instrument, fixing a computer, or cooking a new dish.

My advice is to subscribe to good-quality channels related to your interest and let YouTube recommendations do the rest. The personal recommendations below (out of more than 200 channels that I subscribe to) are closely related to the categories outlined earlier (science, distinguished talks, and how-to):

- AsapSCIENCE[7]: Short videos that use animation (and a good dose of humor) to explain scientific concepts.
- Big Think[8]: a collection of thousands of videos, featuring experts in a broad range of topics, covering "the big ideas and core skills that define knowledge in the 21st century".
- Howcast[9]: vast collection of *how-to* videos covering a wide range of topics, from sewing to playing the guitar, to taking care of a pet rabbit, among many others.

---

[4] http://www.engadget.com/.

[5] http://www.gatesnotes.com/.

[6] http://www.ted.com/.

[7] http://www.youtube.com/user/AsapSCIENCE.

[8] http://www.youtube.com/user/bigthink.

[9] http://www.youtube.com/user/Howcast.

- SciShow[10]: short videos, quiz shows and talk shows on popular science topics.
- Talks at Google[11]: Usually long (45 min or longer) talks by some of the world's best-known book authors, innovators, scientists, actors, actresses, artists, filmmakers, musicians, and speakers.
- TED-Ed[12]: library of animations and educational videos, linked to lesson plans and additional resources available at the TED-Ed website (http://ed.ted.com).

Google (Beyond Search)

Using the Google search engine to locate relevant information has become second-nature to all of us: whenever we want to learn about something quickly we just "google" it. Not many people know that—in addition to its flagship product, the search engine—Google also has a variety of products and sites worth checking out for learning purposes. Some of them are listed below:

- Google Books[13]: Collection of millions of searchable full-text e-books. It also allows signed-in users to create a personalized library of books, organized in bookshelves, which can be shared with friends by making bookshelves publicly visible and sharing the secret library URL.
- Google Cultural Institute[14]: A cultural project that allows visitors to discover exhibits and collections from museums and archives all around the world.
- Google Earth (and beyond!)[15]: Google Earth allows users to explore almost every corner of our planet in great detail. It is available as Web-based, desktop, and mobile app. It has also been expanded to allow exploring the sky, the moon, and planet Mars!
- Google Scholar[16]: Google Scholar provides an easy way to search for scholarly literature—such as journal articles, academic theses, books, abstracts and patents—from a variety of sources, such as: academic publishers, professional societies, online repositories, universities and other websites.
- Google Trends[17]: Google Trends shows—based on Google searches—what are the current trending topics on the Web, organized by country and category. Moreover, using Google Correlate (https://www.google.com/trends/correlate), one can examine search patterns which correspond with real-world trends,

---

[10]http://www.youtube.com/user/scishow.

[11]http://www.youtube.com/user/AtGoogleTalks.

[12]http://www.youtube.com/user/TEDEducation.

[13]http://books.google.com/.

[14]http://www.google.com/culturalinstitute/u/0/home.

[15]http://www.google.com/earth/explore/products/.

[16]http://scholar.google.com/.

[17]http://www.google.com/trends/.

and learn, for example, that user uploaded activity for "Winter Wave" and United States Web Search activity for "Italian wedding soup" have a very high correlation ($r = 0.9374$).

2.5.2 Structured Learning

The Web has also become the destination for structured, formal education. Fully online undergraduate and graduate programs in a wide range of subject areas are now being offered by many universities worldwide. Additionally, the Web became the platform that enabled the rise of massive open online courses (MOOCs), open-access courses available to an audience of (hundreds of) thousands of students that can take courses with some of the world's top-experts covering the latest developments in their fields, for free (or—in some cases—for a modest fee, significantly smaller than tuition at a regular American college or university).

Since the blossoming of the MOOCs movement in late 2011, several MOOC providers have emerged and partnered with prestigious universities worldwide, among them: Coursera[18] (whose partners include Johns Hopkins, U of Michigan, Stanford, Duke, and UC San Diego), Udacity[19] (which offers access to individual Georgia Tech Online Masters in Computer Science), and edX[20] [whose partners include MIT, Harvard, UC Berkeley, and TU Delft (The Netherlands)].

A Checklist

The amount of (mostly free) open-access structured courses—taught by subject matter experts using the latest technological resources—is vast and ever-growing. Before you begin searching for a course, in order to avoid getting caught in the "information overload" trap, I suggest assessing your needs, expectations, and learning style by asking yourself the following questions:

1. What *exactly* do you want to learn? Try to be as precise as possible. For example: you may want to become a front-end Web developer (which could be achieved by taking a series of small courses, in what is called a specialization or "nanodegree") or learn a specific language, tool, or framework within the domain of front-end Web development, such as HTML5, CSS, Bootstrap, or jQuery.
2. What is your learning style? Each individual has a unique learning style and set of preferences, such as loosely structured versus strictly sequential. Moreover, depending on the subject, you may learn more effectively by reading, watching, or actually doing something—building a website, for example.

---

[18]http://www.coursera.org/.
[19]http://www.udacity.com/.
[20]http://www.edx.org/.

3. Is this a continuous process or a one-shot experience? The answer to this question might determine the nature and duration of the learning process, as well as the format and amount of time and money you are willing to invest in it.

Once you have reached satisfactory answers to these diagnostic questions, consider how important are the aspects in the checklist below:

- **Self-paced or not**: self-paced courses (as opposed to courses with rigid start and end dates) allow you to adjust your progress to your available time and learning style, without the pressure of deadlines. The downsides of self-paced courses include: the lack of a sense that you are part of a cohort (taking the same course at the same time as many other students) and the higher risk of delaying your progress due to procrastination.
- **A sense of community**: online learning can be much more satisfactory when students feel connected to other students as part of a community of learners. If this is important to you, check which features are available for interacting with other students, how friendly are they, and how much they foster participation.
- **Online help**, e.g. Q&A forums: every user of an online learning platform will need help at some point, whether it is assistance with the subject matter or the use of the platform itself. Moreover, giving and receiving help (within the limits of academic integrity) is a common practice among participants in online courses.
- **Badges** and other "bragging rights": many online courses offer mechanisms by which you can share your progress and achievements with fellow classmates and friends outside of the learning platform, e.g., via Twitter or Facebook.
- **Videos**: the use of short, effective, professionally-produced videos has become an essential staple of successful online learning programs. You should expect nothing less from a professional site or course, especially a paid one.
- **Continuous feedback**: many online learning programs include clever ways of providing frequent feedback—and often a much-needed "pat on the back" as you progress throughout the program.
- **Reputation**: check the credentials of the instructor, the associated site and—whenever available—the affiliated university. You might be able to learn about a topic from a world-leading authority in that field!
- **Mobile** friendly: the world has gone mobile and for online learning, the convenience of using your smartphone or tablet should not be neglected. Before committing to a course, ensure that its contents (including videos) work well—and without loss of functionality—on mobile devices.
- **Offline** capabilities: online learners do not always have uninterrupted, cheap, and/or reliable Internet access. The ability to download contents for later (offline) viewing adds great flexibility to the learning experience.
- Official **certificate**: several courses have a paid option whose main difference from the free counterpart is the issuing of an official certificate at course completion time. Take this into account if such a certificate is important to you (for personal and/or professional reasons).
- **Cost**: last, but not least, check the cost of the program and what it covers.

Selected Websites for Lifelong Learners

In addition to Coursera, Udacity, and edX (discussed earlier), these are some personal recommendations:

- Codeschool[21]: excellent site for learning programming, with a balanced combination between professional short videos and interactive hands-on exercises using a rich interface. It contains several courses in a variety of topics and programming languages, structured into learning paths. Users collect points in the challenges and earn badges as they complete each course level, culminating in the course completion badge.
- DuoLingo[22]: the brainchild of brilliant computer scientist (and Carnegie Mellon University Professor) Luis von Ahn, it exemplifies the best in terms of "gamification" of language learning. The (mobile) app design is engaging and the gameplay almost addictive. It contains a growing list of languages and remains free at the time of this writing.
- The Khan Academy[23]: enormously popular with K-12 students, it now contains courses in a wide range of topics in the fields of mathematics, science, computer programming, history, art, and economics, among others. The instruction is mostly video-based and the site is packed with options to quantify and encourage continuous learning: statistics, coaches, badges, challenges, energy points, avatar parts, and more!

Lastly, a good portal to online courses, structured by learning categories (e.g., Academics, Art, Computer Programming, Cooking, eBooks, HowTo + DIY, Languages, and Music) is the *No excuse list*.[24] Definitely worth bookmarking!

2.6 Practical Recommendations

2.6.1 Browser

It is important to know that not all websites work on every browser (and there is usually very little you can do about it). Moreover, some browsers are—indeed— better than others, for reasons that are too technical to explain in this introductory text.

Here are some browser-related recommendations:

---

[21] http://www.codeschool.com.

[22] http://www.duolingo.com.

[23] http://www.khanacademy.org.

[24] http://noexcuselist.com/.

- Install two or more leading browsers (e.g., Chrome, Safari, Firefox, Opera). Having a second option may be a lifesaver when a site misbehaves in your favorite browser.
- Keep your browsers updated to the latest version (this can be done automatically).
- Beware of Internet Explorer (IE), especially older versions, since they are notorious for not being compatible with may Web-based standards.
- Remember that "it takes two to tango" (i.e., not all sites run on all browsers).

2.6.2 Browser Extensions (Add-ons)

If you use Google Chrome,[25] Safari,[26] Opera[27] or Mozilla Firefox[28] as your primary browser, you should consider installing additional pieces of software, known as *extensions* or *add-ons*, which allow you to improve and customize the browsing experience.

Some examples of useful extensions include:

- **Ad blockers**, such as Adblock Plus,[29] minimize the number of intrusive ads associated with viewing Web pages. Be mindful, however, that certain sites might require that you disable the ad blocker in order to work properly.
- **Password managers**, such as 1Password,[30] assist you when filling out forms and encourage the healthy habit of using different passwords for different sites.
- **Security- and privacy-related extensions** such as Ghostery[31] can help you control how much information you might be unwilling sending to tracking sites, among other things.
- **Productivity and workflow assistants**—such as Evernote Web clipper, Feedly, Wunderlist, Save to Pocket—allow for a seamless integration between your browser and some of your favorite productivity and note-taking tools and apps.

2.6.3 Safe Browsing

Despite its convenience, the Web has also brought about several privacy and security concerns, from hacker attacks to ID theft, among many others. After all, as the dog

---

[25]http://chrome.google.com/webstore/category/extensions.

[26]http://safari-extensions.apple.com.

[27]http://addons.opera.com/en/extensions/.

[28]http://addons.mozilla.org/en-US/firefox/.

[29]http://adblockplus.org.

[30]http://1password.com.

[31]http://www.ghostery.com.

sitting in front of the computer in the classic 1993 *The New Yorker* cartoon by Peter Steiner famously said to the other dog: "On the Internet, nobody knows you're a dog".

Here are some privacy and security recommendations:

- Install HTTPS Everywhere,[32] a Firefox, Chrome, and Opera extension that encrypts your communications with many major websites, making your browsing more secure.
- Do not volunteer unnecessary information.
- Do not accept cookies from strangers.
- Do not allow sites to track your physical location (unless absolutely necessary).

2.6.4 Speed Test

If you need to check the current speed of your Internet connection consider using http://www.speedtest.net (or its mobile app, available for download at the same Website). It might help explain why certain pages are taking longer than usual to load and—in the case of Internet access from your home—it could assist you on checking whether the actual speed (bit rate) is commensurate with the one you signed up for with your ISP.

2.7 Concluding Remarks

In this chapter we discussed the World Wide Web, from its conception to current use. We paid special attention to the use of the Web as a platform for lifelong learning and offered many suggestions of sites and practical recommendations for a safe, meaningful and effective online experience.

Takeaways from this chapter:

- The Web is here to stay. It is not a fad and will not go away.
- Originally conceived for sharing documents, the Web has become a platform for hosting apps that cover virtually every area of human activity.
- For the past 10 years, we have all become content creators, whether we do it explicitly (e.g., by maintaining a blog) or implicitly (every time we rate, like, or share an item).

(continued)

---

[32]https://www.eff.org/https-everywhere.

- The Web is possibly the best place to learn about any topic.
- The Web browsing experience can be improved by using the right tools (e.g., browsers and selected browser extensions) and adopting measures to protect your privacy and the security of your computer.

References

1. Lee TB (1989) Information management: a proposal. Technical Report, CERN
2. Markoff J (1993) A free and simple computer link.   http://www.nytimes.com/1993/12/08/business/business-technology-a-free-and-simple-computer-link.html?pagewanted=all
3. Merriam Webster (2015) Definition of world wide web. http://www.merriam-webster.com/dictionary/world
4. Pew Research Center (2014) World wide web timeline. http://www.pewinternet.org/2014/03/11/world-wide-web-timeline/
5. Wikipedia (2016) Wikipedia. https://en.wikipedia.org/wiki/Wikipedia

Chapter 3
Smartphones

Abstract The evolution of telephone communication networks and the pervasiveness of cell phones have changed our lives forever. Contemporary smartphones (and associated apps) make all the knowledge in the world available at our fingertips, anywhere, all the time. In this chapter we present an overview of the current state of the art in the smartphone arena, as well as suggestions of useful apps.

3.1 The Pervasiveness of Cell Phones

Cell phones have become an integral part of our daily lives, to a point that 29 % of cell owners describe their cell phone as "something they can't imagine living without [15]". Another often-cited statistics claims that there are more cell phones than toothbrushes in use in our planet today. If we broaden the field to include other gadgets with communication capabilities (e.g., tablets), the number of gadgets on Earth has surpassed the planet's population since October 2014 [14]. In other words, if you're reading this, I can predict with almost certainty that you own one or more mobile devices.

In this book we are particularly interested in a subclass of cell phones known as *smartphones*. A legitimate question to ask, then, is: "What, exactly, is a smartphone?" The answer would probably look like this: "A smartphone is a portable computing device which extends the features of a cell phone, by adding capabilities originally present in other mobile devices, such as personal digital assistant (PDA), media player and GPS navigation unit." Most smartphones have high-quality cameras, powerful processors, Internet access capabilities, color high-resolution displays, and a touchscreen user interface. But the key aspect of what makes a cell phone a smartphone is their ability to run specialized application programs, known simply as *apps*.

The smartphone market has grown exponentially in the past 10 years. This growth has been driven by several factors, such as:

- **Powerful and relatively inexpensive hardware.** As famed scientist Michio Kaku stated in his 2012 book *Physics of the Future*: "Today, your cell phone has more computer power than all of NASA back in 1969 when it sent two astronauts to the moon" [13].

- **Social networks.** Smartphone users spend a significant amount of their time (24 % or more, depending on the statistics) using social network apps. No other app category comes even close. This realization led to the development of the HTC First, also known as "the Facebook phone", which—for several technical and economical reasons [3]—did not succeed.
- **Improving telecommunication infrastructure.** The growth of cellular data networks with increasing bandwidth (3G, 4G, LTE), combined with the increasing availability of Wi-Fi hotspots, numerous satellites orbiting the planet, and almost ubiquitous access to GPS have enabled a scenario where 24/7 connectivity is a reality.
- **Many useful apps!** The popularity of smartphones is intrinsically connected to the increasing availability of mobile apps, a topic that will be expanded upon in Sect. 3.5.

3.2 Interesting Statistics

In this section I have compiled a few recent statistics that show how pervasive, ever-growing, and irreversible the smartphone revolution is.

3.2.1 Time Spent on the Smartphone

Millennials (18–24-year-old users) spend more than 90 h per month on their smartphone apps, and usage declines with age: for users age 65 and higher the number is 40 h per month. Tablet app engagement is much lower (40 h per month or less), but generally increases with age outside of the 18–24 year-old segment; this may be explained by many factors, such as use of e-readers, appreciation for larger screens, and usage of tablets as replacements for a desktop or laptop computer, which are more prevalent in older age groups [5]. Smartphone users spend 7 out of 8 min on apps—the remaining time is shared by other activities, such as mobile Web browsing, texting, and making/receiving phone calls [4].

3.2.2 Most Popular Apps

There are more than 100 mobile apps whose audiences are in the range of millions of unique visitors, and this number continues to grow (the growth was by 24 % or higher between June 2014 and June 2015). At the top of the list: Facebook (the most popular app, by far, by any measure), YouTube, and Facebook

Messenger.[1] Moreover, 78 % of the time using smartphone apps are spent on the smartphone user's Top three apps, despite the average smartphone user visiting 25 apps per month [5].

3.2.3   Organizing and Accessing Apps

When asked "Which factors, if any, influence your decision to move any of your apps to your home screen?", 46 % of the users answered "How often I use the app", followed by "Easier access" (44 %), "I often need to access the app quickly" (32 %), and "My interest in that app or kind of app" (21 %) [5]. Interestingly enough, only 1 out of 5 smartphone users made no effort to customize which apps appear on their home screen, which suggests that "app usage is a reflexive, habitual behavior where those occupying the best home screen real estate are used most frequently" [5]. In fact, 73 % of smartphone users keep their most frequently used app in their home screen (and, interestingly enough, less than 8 % of the users—most of them millennials—organize their apps into folders) [5].

3.2.4   App Categories

The three most popular app categories—based on share of mobile app time spent— are: Social Networking (29 %), Radio (15 %), and Games (11 %) [5].

3.2.5   Social and Entertainment Apps

Social apps such as Facebook and Twitter have become the primary platform for users to stay informed on news, culture, and their family and friends' personal and professional updates. Entertainment apps—including a sub-genre known as "casual games" (which includes Candy Crush, Words with Friends, and Clash of Clans, among others)—benefit from the occasional pockets of free time that users experience throughout the day. Millennials spend an average of 2 h per day on social and entertainment apps; this number drops by half for users age 55 and up [5].

---

[1] Eight of the Top 10 apps are owned by Facebook or Google [5].

3.2.6 A Trip Down Memory Lane

Timehop, an app that allows users to explore what they were doing on the same date on social media (such as Facebook, Instagram, and Twitter) has experienced an explosive growth in terms of daily (921 %) and monthly (651 %) usage between June 2014 and June 2015 [5]. After seeing Timehop hit six million daily users on mobile, Facebook launched in March 2015 a competing feature called "On This Day"[2] [6].

3.2.7 Messaging

The messaging category experienced a substantial boost (mostly outside of the U.S.) with Facebook's unbundling of FB Messenger (332 % growth in number of unique visitors between June 2013 and June 2015 [5]) and the explosive growth of WhatsApp, which recently reached one billion users [20].

3.2.8 Changes in Daily Habits

Our increasing dependency on smartphones has led to some amusing—and occasionally worrying—statistics, as well. Here are some examples:

- 67 % of cell owners find themselves checking their phone for messages, alerts, or calls—even when they don't notice their phone ringing or vibrating [15]. The so-called *phantom vibration syndrome* is being seriously studied by researchers in the field of psychology of human behavior (see [7] for an example).
- 44 % of cell owners have slept with their phone next to their bed because they wanted to make sure they didn't miss any calls, text messages, or other updates during the night [15].
- In the U.S., people check news on their phones 40 times per day, 88 % of consumers use their mobile device while watching TV, and 75 % bring their smartphones to the bathroom [2].

3.3 Staying in Touch

A smartphone (or any phone for that matter!) should serve a primary purpose: communicating with other people through voice, (and, increasingly more each day,) text and video. In addition to regular phone conversations and text (SMS)

---

[2]https://www.facebook.com/onthisday.

messaging, these are some of the most popular apps and technologies for one-on-one (or small group) communications in use today:

- **Facebook Messenger:** extremely popular Facebook app that supports voice and video calls (in addition to text messaging) among its 900 million active users [16].
- **FaceTime:** a videotelephony app developed by Apple that enables real-time audio and video communication among Apple devices (only) such as iPhones and iPads. FaceTime supports conference calls for audio only.
- **Google Hangouts:** supports messaging, voice and video calls (including conference calls for up to ten users) among Google users.
- **Skype:** arguably the most popular app[3] for voice and video communications among users worldwide. Skype also supports conference calls, text messaging as well as file transfers, among other features. It is available on most devices, supported by a freemium model, which includes options such as SkypeOut, an affordable way to make international calls to mobiles and landlines.
- **WhatsApp:** an increasingly popular app originally created (in 2009) to provide carrier-independent text messaging services. Today, in addition to text messaging, WhatsApp users can make voice calls as well send images, video, and audio to other users using standard cellular mobile numbers. WhatsApp is available on most smartphones and used by a billion people, more than 10 % of which reside in Brazil, where it has become the de facto standard app for one-to-one and group communications. It was purchased by Facebook in 2014 for $19 Billion USD.

Besides the apps mentioned above, smartphone users can also stay in touch by using the *direct (private) message* or *chat* option of many popular apps (such as Instagram and Twitter) and games (such as SongPop or Words with Friends).

3.4 iPhone, Android, or Other?

In this section we take a brief look at the key features of the leading types of smartphones, the Apple iPhone[4] and Android-based smartphones.[5] Together they correspond to a 98.4 % marketshare worldwide, whereas Windows Phone and Blackberry, combined, have a paltry 1.3 % marketshare [10].

Deciding which phone to purchase is a complex decision driven by many factors, such as: software compatibility, app availability, user friendliness, richness of features, hardware capabilities, "cool factor", and cost, among others. It is, ultimately, a very personal decision and there are not enough compelling technical reasons to prefer iPhone over Android-based smartphones (or vice-versa). Even so, in Table 3.1 I present a very brief summary of pros and cons of the two biggest players in the smartphone race.

---

[3]300 million active users as of April 2016 [16].

[4]http://www.apple.com/iphone/.

[5]http://www.android.com/phones/.

Table 3.1 iPhone vs. Android

	Apple iPhone (iOS)	Android[a]
App store	Two million apps (as of June 2016)[17]	2.2 million apps (as of June 2016) [17]
App security	Very secure (apps undergo very strict approval process before they are made available in the Apple App Store)	Less secure app approval process, which requires additional attention from the user before installing (potentially malicious) apps
Cost	Apple products are, admittedly, rather expensive, possibly as a result of their incredible brand-name recognition	Usually more affordable than iPhone
Ecosystem	Apple's ecosystem (iTunes, iCloud, etc.) is a walled garden	Open ecosystem, allowing many apps, products and services to compete
Hardware	Apple only	Confusing hardware choices (multiple manufacturers—such as Samsung, HTC, Motorola, Amazon, LG, and Sony—and versions)
Operating system (OS)	The latest version of Apple's iOS is supported by relatively new (3 years or less) devices	Many different versions of Android, whose support varies from one manufacturer/model to the next

[a](multiple manufacturers)

3.5 Apps

Ever since the introduction of Apple's iPhone 3G in 2009, the catchphrase "There's an app for that" (trademarked by Apple in 2010) has become ubiquitous. Mobile app development has taken off and provided a wonderful new platform for creative software designers to create useful (and occasionally revolutionary) apps, which leverage the ever-increasing hardware capabilities of smartphones and address just about every aspect of human life. It is not an exaggeration to say that we can do just about everything with a smartphone (and properly chosen apps) these days.

The problem is: how to select the best apps from millions of options (see Table 3.1) available either in the Apple App Store or the Google Play Store?

The large number of apps and the speed at which new apps are developed make it impossible for a "static" publication (such as this book) to stay current with the latest and greatest offerings in each category. Rather than engaging in this (ultimately futile) exercise, in this section I will describe the main app categories and suggest references for searching for news and reviews of associated apps.

Table 3.2 shows some of the main categories under which app stores (such as Apple's App store and Google Play store) organize their offerings. This classification is not a rigorous taxonomy, but simply a way to make it easier to know where to look when researching potentially useful apps for your device.

A good way to use Table 3.2 is to ask yourself three questions:

1. What do I *really* want to do with a smartphone?
2. How much do I want to pay for a certain app?
3. How do I know if it's any good?

Table 3.2 App categories

Category	Contents	Representative apps
Books	Audiobook players, eBook readers, apps to access your (public) library catalog, share what you're reading with others, and more	Kindle, Audible, Wattpad, Nook, Overdrive, Goodreads, Scribd
Business and Productivity	PDF readers, scanners, scheduling, job search, email, and productivity apps, among others	GoodReader, Evernote, HotSchedules, Scanner Pro, Gmail, Dropbox, Pushbullet, LinkedIn Job Search
Education	Broad range of apps for all ages and topics, including both informal and structured/formal learning as well as "brain training" games	iTunes U, Coursera, YouTube, Khan Academy, Duolingo, Mathway, Skyview, Peak, Lumosity, Brainwell, Elevate
Entertainment	A very large and broad category that includes apps related to movie streaming as well as reviews, tickets, and much more	Netflix, Fandango, IMDb, Hulu, Amazon Instant Video, HBO NOW, iFunny
Finance	Personal banking, business expense tracker, investment and financial advice, stocks, and more	Mint, PayPal, Credit Karma, Mile IQ, Acorns
Food and Drink	Restaurant guides, grocery shopping, recipes, etc.	Yelp, Open Table, Vivino, Untappd, Starbucks, Allrecipes, Forks Over Knives
Games	(By far) the largest [1] (and most profitable [19]) category of apps. Includes games for every age range and gaming style	Candy Crush Saga, Clash of Clans, Angry Birds, Mobile Strike, Minecraft Pocket Edition, Subway Surfers, slither.io, Words with Friends
Health and fitness	Food, nutrition, sleep, health trackers, running, cycling, and more	My Fitness Pal, FitBit, Zova, LoseIt!, Sleepio, Strava, Runkeeper
Lifestyle	Broad range of apps, including house searching, remodeling, and decorating, car buying, journaling, and beauty salons, among others	Zillow, Trulia, TrueCar, Day One, Angie's List, Real Simple, StyleSeat
Medical	Medical advice, health monitoring, personal care apps, and more	Mayo Clinic, WebMD, GoodRx, Epocrates, Medscape
Music	Apps to learn, discover, play, and listen to music	Pandora, Spotify, Shazam, SoundCloud, Magic Piano, Sing! Karaoke, Cadenza
Navigation	Maps and navigation systems, public transit, private transportation	Google Maps, Apple Maps, Citymapper, Waze, Uber, Lyft
News	Magazines, newspapers, TV networks, and other news sources	NYTimes, Apple News, BBC News, Twitter, Reddit, BuzzFeed, The Wall Street Journal

(continued)

Table 3.2 (continued)

Category	Contents	Representative apps
Photo and video	Apps for creating, editing, discovering, organizing, and sharing visual media	Instagram, Snapchat, YouTube, 500px, Vimeo, VSCO, Facetune, Afterlight, Snapseed
Reference	Encyclopedias, dictionaries, atlases, language translators, and more	Merriam-Webster dictionary, Google Translate, Wolfram Alpha, Wikipedia Mobile, Google Earth
Social network	Messaging, blogs, communities, online dating, and other social apps	Facebook, WhatsApp, Facebook Messenger, Twitter, Instagram, Pinterest, Kik, Skype, Tumblr, Periscope, Vine, Snapchat, Path, LinkedIn, Tinder, eHarmony
Sports	Sports scores, news, publications, teams, competitions, tickets, and more	ESPN, Fox Sports GO, Gametime, theScore, Sports Illustrated
Travel	Apps for planning, booking, and improving your traveling experience	Kayak, GateGuru, TripAdvisor, Airbnb, National Parks
Weather	Forecasts and alerts	The Weather Channel, NOAA Weather Radar, Dark Sky, Earthquake

The answer to question 1 will probably take you to the right categories in Table 3.2, from where you could use the listed apps as initial suggestions.

Answering question 2 is a bit harder, since it depends a lot on the app, what it is for, and its competitors. Moreover, the cost of an app is not always known in advance. Many app makers use a "freemium" business model, where the basic app (usually with limited functionality) is offered for free, but additional features come at a price. Additionally, many apps (especially games) include so-called *in-app purchases* (for items such as game currency), which may lead to spending significantly more money during the lifetime of the app than its nominal price at the app store.

Finally, the best way to get an answer to question 3 is to look at the reviews at the corresponding app store or reputable tech blogs and sites. App developers keep a close eye on reviews, especially negative ones. Since app stores typically display results for the *latest version* by default, it is not uncommon for app developers to push a new version (ideally, but not necessarily, fixing bugs that prompted the negative reviews) even if it is just a way to "reset" the review results (and grades, in number of stars) for the latest version (the one they just made available at the app store).

3.6 Privacy and Security

In this section we have compiled a few basic recommendations to protect your privacy and increase your security while using your smartphone.[6]

- Learn how to use your smartphone's privacy settings. Consult official online documentation for your specific smartphone and operating system (iOS or Android) version and get acquainted with all the available options. It is quite possible that some default settings are *not* of your liking; you should learn how to change them as soon as you get a new device or perform an OS update.
- Set up two-factor authentication, a method that requires a combination of two of these: something that you *know* (such as a passcode), something that you *have* (such as your actual device), and/or something that you *are* (such as your fingerprint). This should stop hackers from accessing your data even if they get to know your username and password.
- Turn off most notifications! Notifications can come in many variations—for example, text-only (vs. text-and-sound), visible on the lock screen (or not). Most app developers will try to convince you that you should allow their apps to send notifications and, to be fair, in some cases it makes sense—for example, if you use apps to remind you periodically to take a break and go for a short walk.[7] But why do you need to be notified every time one of your friends posts something on Facebook, likes a photo you posted on Instagram, or retweets one of your recent tweets?

   Being constantly interrupted by notifications is a modern affliction. One of the major problems of allowing apps to send us notifications is that such notifications may come at inappropriate times, without considering the task you might be engaged in (and what such task demands). Recent studies show that answering notifications impedes task performance and the ability to resume to the original task at hand [12]; moreover, even just knowing that one has received a notification can negatively impact sustained attention [18].
- Prevent (previews of) messages and emails from appearing on the lock screen, which could potentially allow anyone with access to your (locked) device to catch a glimpse of their contents. On a related note, you should also consider limiting what actions can be performed without a passcode, such as replying to your messages—which, surprisingly enough, is turned on by default on the iPhone.
- Prevent apps from uploading your data. When an app wants your data (for example, access to contacts, email, calendar, and photos), either for processing or uploading, it will usually ask for your permission when you first set up the app.

---

[6]Most of the recommendations listed here are iPhone-specific [8], but they address privacy and security concerns that are common to all smartphone users. For Android-specific recommendations, check [9].

[7]See http://goo.gl/7g3xRZ for a list of apps in that category.

You should learn how to review these settings (in case you did not pay enough attention when you first granted those apps permission) and, maybe, revoke them. Note, however, that if you have already granted an app access to your data, switching off the service on your device does not mean that service will delete your data. You will have to contact that company or app maker for this.

- Beware of apps that track your location (even in the background)! You should only grant permission to access your location to apps that absolutely need it in order to perform their job (such as Google Maps) and only while you are using the app. By doing so, you know that once you close/dismiss the app, its ability to track your location stops as well.
- Similarly, you should only grant access to your device's camera and/or microphone to a certain app if those devices are absolutely necessary for the app to work—such as Skype or WhatsApp, for example.
- If you have an iPhone, enable Apple's *Find My iPhone* [11]. It can be extremely valuable if your device gets lost or stolen. Find My iPhone can display on a map the current location of your device. It allows you to locate, lock, or erase your iPhone and prevents it from being erased or reactivated without your password. Additionally, by selecting *Send Last Location*, your device will update Apple's servers with the last location when the battery is critically low, just before it powers down.
- Require password with every app purchase in the Apple App Store. For your financial peace of mind, you might want to ensure that each app requires your Apple ID or your fingerprint. This should prevent multiple purchases being made on the credit card on file, after your initial authorization.
- Consider installing a content blocker[8] (a feature introduced in iOS 9). These apps not only work as "ad-blockers" (preventing intrusive ads from displaying and, consequently, slowing down your browsing experience), but they also stop privacy-invading ad cookies from tracking you.
- Set the auto-lock option to the shortest possible time, thereby reducing the chances of someone inadvertently accessing your device without it requiring a passcode.

Takeaways from this chapter:

- Smartphones have changed our lives forever. In addition to allowing multiple ways to communicate using voice, text, and video, smartphones make all the knowledge in the world available at our fingertips, anywhere, anytime.

(continued)

---

[8] See http://goo.gl/G8cf7g for a list of recommended content blocker apps for iOS.

- Thanks to their powerful and feature-rich hardware and an enormous (and ever-growing) number of associated apps, smartphones have replaced multiple devices—such as cellphone, camera, navigation system, health monitor and more—and consolidated them into one.
- When deciding upon which device to purchase, the decision has come down to either the Apple iPhone or (one of many) Android-based smartphones, since the two platforms, combined, have more than 98 % of the marketshare worldwide.
- Modern smartphones have also become a platform for app developers. In today's app stores you can find millions of apps for virtually everything!
- It is impossible to be 100 % current with the latest and greatest apps, but there are good sources of news and reviews that can assist you in selecting (and occasionally replacing) apps in different categories.
- Smartphone users should learn how to adjust their device's privacy and security settings.

References

1. Apple: most popular app store categories 2016 — statistic. http://www.statista.com/statistics/270291/popular-categories-in-the-app-store/. Accessed 26 June 2016
2. Bennett S (2014) Social media, internet, sms, apps – incredible smartphone stats, facts and figures. http://www.adweek.com/socialtimes/golden-age-mobile/497954
3. Cheng R (2013) Here's why the Facebook phone flopped. http://www.cnet.com/news/heres-why-the-facebook-phone-flopped/
4. comScore (2014) The U.S. mobile app report. http://www.comscore.com/Insights/Presentations-and-Whitepapers/2014/The-US-Mobile-App-Report,
5. comScore (2015) The 2015 U.S. mobile app report. http://www.comscore.com/Insights/Presentations-and-Whitepapers/2015/The-2015-US-Mobile-App-Report
6. Constine J (2015) Facebook's timehop clone "on this day" shows you your posts from years ago. http://techcrunch.com/2015/03/24/facehop/
7. Drouin M, Kaiser DH, Miller DA (2012) Phantom vibrations among undergraduates: prevalence and associated psychological characteristics. Comput Hum Behav 28(4):1490–1496
8. For privacy and security, change these ios 9 settings right now — zdnet. http://www.zdnet.com/pictures/ios-9-iphone-ipad-privacy-security-settings/6/. Accessed 25 June 2016
9. For privacy and security, change these android settings right now — zdnet. http://www.zdnet.com/pictures/android-phone-tablet-privacy-security-settings/. Accessed 25 June 2016
10. Gartner (2016) Market share: devices, all countries, 4Q15 update
11. icloud - find my iphone, ipad, and mac. - apple. https://www.apple.com/icloud/find-my-iphone.html. Accessed 25 June 2016
12. Iqbal ST, Horvitz E (2010) Notifications and awareness: a field study of alert usage and preferences. In: Proceedings of the 2010 ACM conference on computer supported cooperative work, CSCW '10. ACM, New York, pp 27–30
13. Kaku M (2011) Physics of the future: how science will shape human destiny and our daily lives by the year 2100. Doubleday, New York

14. Mack E (2014) There are now more gadgets on Earth than people. http://www.cnet.com/news/ there-are-now-more-gadgets-on-earth-than-people/
15. Pew Research Center (2014) Mobile technology fact sheet. http://www.pewinternet.org/fact-sheets/mobile-technology-fact-sheet/
16. Statista (2016) Leading social networks worldwide as of April 2016, ranked by number of active users (in millions). http://www.statista.com/statistics/272014/global-social-networks-ranked-by-number-of-users/
17. Statista (2016) Number of apps available in leading app stores as of June 2016. http://www.statista.com/statistics/276623/number-of-apps-available-in-leading-app-stores/
18. Stothart C, Mitchum A, Yehnert C (2015) The attentional cost of receiving a cell phone notification. J Exp Psychol Hum Percept Perform 41(4):893
19. Top grossing iPhone games 2016 — Statistic. http://goo.gl/3oN0to. Accessed 26 June 2016
20. WhatsApp Blog (2016) One billion. htts://blog.whatsapp.com/616/One-billion

Chapter 4
Social Networks

Abstract Social networks are one of the greatest phenomena of the twenty-first century. In this chapter we examine social networking websites (and apps) and their users. After presenting essential statistics from recent studies, we focus on the most popular social networks (Facebook and Twitter) and discuss their history, jargon, usage, and impact. The chapter contains many practical recommendations for using a selected set of social networks most effectively and following the proper etiquette.

4.1 The Social Network Phenomenon

Social networks have been at the center of many social changes and technological advances of the twenty-first century. The rise of social media has impacted work, politics, communications patterns, as well as the way people consume and share information about virtually every topic [13].

If you are reading this book, it is quite likely that you have an account (and use regularly) one or more of these: Facebook, Twitter, LinkedIn, and Instagram, to name but a few.

But what, exactly, is a social network? According to Google, a social network can be[1]:

1. a network of social interactions and personal relationships.
2. a dedicated website or other application that enables users to communicate with each other by posting information, comments, messages, images, etc.

Social networks can be established at multiple levels and for different purposes, such as: work, school, friends, family, events, forums, clubs, church, etc. It is hard to determine how many social networking websites are currently active[2] or to measure their impact and popularity.

---

[1]http://www.google.com/search?q=social+network+definition.

[2]According to a list at [10], there are at least 19... starting with the letter 'F'. Interestingly enough, Wikipedia also maintains a list of (20, and growing) 'defunct social networking sites' [9].

© The Author(s) 2016

O. Marques, *Innovative Technologies in Everyday Life*, SpringerBriefs
in Computer Science, DOI 10.1007/978-3-319-45699-7_4

Many social networks cater to specific aspects of human life, such as professional connections and opportunities (LinkedIn[3]), image sharing (Instagram[4]), video sharing (Vine[5]), location sharing through "checkins" (Swarm, by Foursquare[6]), visual bookmarking (Pinterest[7]), or real-time rich messaging (WhatsApp.[8])

4.1.1   Usage Facts and Statistics

Who uses social networks? Why? For how many hours a day? These and many other questions are being frequently asked by researchers and statisticians everywhere. Here are some interesting facts and figures.

According to a recent report by the Pew Research Center [13] focused on the US[9]:

- **Overall usage:** 65 % of American adults use social networking sites, up from 7 % in 2005.
- **Age differences:** Unsurprisingly, young adults (ages 18–29) are the most likely to use social media—90 % do. However, usage among senior citizens (65 and older) has skyrocketed: today, 35 % of them report using social media, compared with only 2 % 10 years ago.
- **Racial and ethnic homogeneity:** There are no significant differences among racial or ethnic groups, since 65 % of whites, 65 % of Hispanics and 56 % of African-Americans currently use social media.
- **Education:** Americans who have attended college (partially, at least) are more likely than those with a high school diploma or less to use social media, a trend that has been consistent since 2005.

For a global perspective, these are some recent facts and figures from Statista[10]:

- There are 2.04 billion social network users worldwide, up from 0.97 billion in 2010. This number is expected to grow to 2.55 billion in 2018 [12].

---

[3]http://www.linkedin.com/.

[4]http://instagram.com/.

[5]http://vine.co/.

[6]http://www.swarmapp.com/.

[7]http://pinterest.com/.

[8]http://www.whatsapp.com/.

[9]"This analysis of social media usage is based on a compilation of 27 surveys and about 47,000 interviews among adult internet users and about 62,000 interviews among all adults conducted by Pew Research Center from March 2005 to July 2015." [13].

[10]http://www.statista.com.

- User engagement continues to grow: as of the fourth quarter of 2014, the average daily time spent on social networks by users in the United States was almost 3 h. The global average is 101.4 min per day surfing social networks [15].
- As of April 2016, the top-three social networks (by number of users) are: Facebook (1.59 billion), WhatsApp (one billion), and Facebook Messenger (900 million) [3].

4.2 Facebook

Facebook is the largest, most famous, and most popular social network platform in existence. It was created by Mark Zuckerberg in 2004, when he was a sophomore at Harvard University. During the past 12 years, it has grown to become *the* global social network, with more than 1.5 billion users worldwide.

These are some of Facebook's historical milestones (see [5, 6, 18] for more):

- October 2005: Facebook Photos are introduced.[11]
- April 2006: Facebook becomes available on mobile devices.[12]
- May 2007: Facebook launches Platform, a software development environment that allows outside programmers to develop tools for sharing photos, taking quizzes and playing games. The Platform system gives rise to a *Facebook economy* and enables the success of companies such as game maker Zynga Inc.,[13] the company behind *Farmville* and *Words with Friends*, among many other bestselling titles [18].
- April 2008: Facebook Chat launches [18].
- February 2009: Facebook introduces *Like*, allowing people to endorse other people's posts[14] [18].
- June 2009: Facebook surpasses Myspace[15] as the leading online social network in the US [18].
- August 2010: Facebook launches location feature, allowing people to share where they are with their friends through checkins [18].
- October 2010: *The Social Network* movie—centered around Zuckerberg and the legal battles over Facebook's founding—is released. It would win three Academy Awards [18].
- July 2011: Facebook partners with Skype to add video chat and updates its website interface to make messaging more seamless [6].

---

[11]Surprisingly enough, the site—until then—mainly consisted of text and personal details about each user [5].Today, more than 350 million images are uploaded to Facebook each day [1].

[12]As of the first quarter of 2016, approximately 894 million Facebook users accessed the social network *exclusively* via mobile device [2].

[13]http://www.zynga.com/.

[14]It is very hard to think of Facebook as we know it today without the iconic *Like* feature.

[15]http://myspace.com/.

Fig. 4.1 Facebook headquarters entrance sign showing the iconic "Like" symbol. Courtesy of Wikimedia Commons

- September 2011: Facebook introduces *Timeline*, a new version of the profile page, meant to show highlights from a user's entire life rather than recent posts [18].
- December 2011: Facebook moves to Menlo Park, Calif. Its address is 1 Hacker Way (Fig. 4.1) [18].
- January 2012: Facebook starts showing advertisements (called *Featured Posts*) in the news feed. The advertisements are generally for pages that one's Facebook friends have engaged with [6].
- April 2012: Facebook acquires Instagram for $1 billion USD [6].
- May 2012: Facebook goes public (IPO), with a share price of $38 apiece, valuing the company at $104 billion USD, the largest valuation to date for a newly listed public company [6].
- October 2012: Facebook reaches one billion active users [18].
- August 2013: Facebook launches Internet.org—in collaboration with six cellphone companies (Samsung, Ericsson, MediaTek, Nokia, Opera, and Qualcomm)—, an initiative that aims to bring affordable Internet access to everybody by increasing affordability, increasing efficiency, and facilitating the development of new business models around the provision of Internet access [6].
- January 2014: Facebook starts to roll out "trending topics", showing users the most popular topics at any given moment [18].

- February 2014: Facebook launches a news app, *Paper*,[16] a separate iOS app that provides a newspaper-like or magazine-like experience for reading on the phone [6].
- February 2014: Facebook announces that it is acquiring the multi-platform mobile messaging app WhatsApp for $16 billion USD; the acquisition would be confirmed in October 2014 [6].
- March 2014: Facebook's face recognition algorithm (*DeepFace* [16]) reaches near-human accuracy in identifying faces [6].
- March 2014: Facebook announces that it is acquiring Oculus VR, Inc., a leading virtual reality company, for $2 billion USD [6].
- July 2014: Facebook launches *Save*, a read-it-later feature that allows users to save links, places, and media pages for later perusal [6].

4.2.1 To Be or Not to Be (on Facebook)

Having a social network presence is a highly personal decision. In the case of Facebook, this decision is made a bit more difficult because in many countries (such as the US) and social circles, many people expect that you have a Facebook account (and keep it fresh with frequent posts and updates). Social pressure on one end and (legitimate) concerns with privacy on the opposite end are two of the clearest driving forces to make a decision on whether to join (and stay in) Facebook. To give you a better and broader range of aspects to keep in mind before deciding, here are some pros and cons of being on Facebook.

Pros

- Everyone I know is on Facebook! Why should I stay out and miss all the excitement?
- Facebook provides an easy way to keep in touch with friends and family, regardless of their physical location.
- Facebook offers several convenient options to share information, from writing new posts (the equivalent of forwarding an email or retweeting a tweet) to sharing privately via Messenger.
- Facebook can be useful as a newsreader, since it allows users to "like" and/or "follow" their favorite sources and offers several options to personalize the news feeds that you might be interested in.
- Facebook also allows you to see the latest news and updates from your favorite brands, shops, restaurants, book authors, etc.

---

[16]http://www.facebook.com/paper/.

- Facebook makes it easy to establish an online presence as a business or professional, through Facebook Pages.[17]
- Many sites, blogs, and apps integrate well with Facebook in (at least) two convenient ways: they offer the option to "login with Facebook" (which—among other advantages—spares you from creating and memorizing another username/password combination) and they make it easy to share items directly from their site (or app) to your Facebook friends and followers.

Cons

- Facebook's privacy settings are somewhat complex and require a fair amount of time and technical knowledge to adjust properly. Moreover, several options are enabled by default and Facebook expects you to opt out, if they violate your desired level of privacy.
- Facebook's revenue come—in part—from (tailored) advertisements. You might have legitimate concerns about how accurate these tailored ads can be and wonder how much do they know about you.
- An *algorithm* decides what you see, when, and how often in your Facebook feed, which can be extremely frustrating. On one hand, you may see too many posts from the same few sources; on the other hand, you risk missing on updates from friends that you care about, because Facebook's algorithms chose to bury such posts beyond an easy reach.[18]
- Social networks in general—and Facebook in particular—makes you wonder: Who, exactly, are my *friends*? Do they care about them equally? Telling apart friends from acquaintances, for example, is not an easy task in Facebook. Contrary to Google+—which makes it easy to assign each of our contacts to one or more *circles* (for example, "poker buddies", "clients", "high-school classmates")—Facebook's alternative (classifying your contacts into separate lists and using the "audience selector" every time you post or share something) is extremely cumbersome. Sooner or later, you will post or share an item to the wrong intended audience.
- There are other (better) options for photo sharing than Facebook. If your interested lies in hosting photos online and sharing them with selected audiences, you might be better off with one of these: Flickr,[19] Google Photos,[20] Smugmug,[21]

---

[17]You are invited to check my professional page at http://www.facebook.com/ProfessorOgeMarques, if you are interested.

[18]The algorithm can be tweaked by 'boosting' or 'promoting' posts, two options that earn additional revenues for Facebook.

[19]http://www.flickr.com/.

[20]http://photos.google.com/.

[21]http://www.smugmug.com/.

imgur,[22] 500px,[23] Dropbox,[24] or Amazon Prime Photos[25] (see Chap. 5 for additional discussions).

As a final note, if—after having read the Pros and Cons above—you have decided that you want to leave Facebook, beware that, even if you *deactivate* your account, they still have your data until you permanently *delete* your account.[26]

4.2.2 Facebook Etiquette

One of the major complaints from Facebook users comes from what they perceive to be poor etiquette from other users. The lists below—compiled from a variety of sources as well as personal experience as a Facebook user for several years—summarize some of the DOs and DON'Ts of Facebook etiquette.[27]

Do

- Be mindful of what you post/like/comment on/share. Once you do it, there is typically no way to undo it without any possible trace or consequence.
- Message private matters instead of posting on someone's wall.
- Reply to comments, especially if they are questions. This shows engagement and demonstrates your interest in establishing conversations.
- Avoid posting comments on every post. If you want to simply express a positive reaction, there is always the *Like* button.
- Be careful of your tone. Written language can always be tricky. Use emoticons (emojis) when appropriate.
- Reply promptly to messages, especially if you are running a professional/business page, since the speed of responses appears quite visibly to your visitors.
- Let your friends know when they've been hacked. If you see a strange post by a friend that you can almost guarantee would never post such things, it probably means that your friend's account has been compromised.

Don't

- Make friend requests to strangers. Follow their (public) updates, instead.

---

[22]http://imgur.com/.

[23]http://500px.com/.

[24]http://www.dropbox.com/.

[25]http://www.amazon.com/clouddrive/primephotos.

[26]See official instructions for properly deleting your Facebook account at https://www.facebook.com/help/224562897555674.

[27]You might also enjoy taking the etiquette quiz at http://goo.gl/LZvyXB.

- Post anything that might hurt you professionally. Even venting about your work may have undesirable negative consequences.
- Overshare.
- Start a flame war.
- Tag your friends in awfully taken (or embarrassing) photos.
- Poke others to get their attention. If you have something meaningful to communicate, send them a direct message, instead.
- Issue meaningless calls to action, for example: "If you want to fight world hunger, put the color of your underwear as your status update for the next half hour. I want to see who is brave enough to take a stand."
- Practice *vaguebooking*, defined as "any update on a social network (although primarily Facebook) that is intentionally vague" [22]. Status updates which fall under the category of vaguebooking can be long or short, but most comprise just a few simple words, for example: "wondering if it is all worth it" or "one day she will regret it".

4.3   Twitter

Twitter is an online social networking service that enables users to send short 140-character messages called *tweets* [20]. As of April 2016, Twitter had 320 million monthly active users, despite being banned in China (which provides alternatives such as Sina Weibo or WeChat) [4]. Registered users can read and post tweets as well as follow other users via update feed [20]. As of June 2016, Katy Perry (@katyperry) was the most-followed celebrity on Twitter with more than 89.5 million followers, with U.S. President Obama (@barackobama) ranking fourth (75.5 million followers) and the official Twitter account (@Twitter) in tenth place (55.2 million followers)[28] [21].

Twitter usage is becoming increasingly prominent during events. This phenomenon, known as *live-tweeting*, allows Twitter users to engage in cultural happenings such as sporting events or television airings, sharing their experiences with others while the event is taking place [20]. This is known as the *second screen* phenomenon: as of January 2014, approximately 61 % of internet users were performing mobile activities such as online surfing or messaging when watching TV [14].

These are some of Twitter's historical milestones (see [11, 19] for more):

- March 2006: Twitter co-founder Jack Dorsey sends the world's first tweet.

---

[28]In an amusing example of how social networks interact with one another, the fifth most popular Twitter account is the official YouTube account (@YouTube), with 61.3 million followers [21]. Incidentally, the Twitter YouTube channel has only 86,000 subscribers.

- August 2007: The hashtag (#), first proposed by user Chris Messina (@chrismessina), debuts on Twitter.
- May 2009: NASA astronaut Mike Massimino becomes the first person to send a tweet from space.
- April 2010: Twitter launches *Promoted Tweets*, which are paid by advertisers and become a revenue source for Twitter.
- December 2010: Twitter plays major role in Arab Spring protests, helping protesters circumvent autocracies and communicate with one another to support mobilization efforts.
- September 2011: Twitter announces 100 million monthly active users, worldwide.
- December 2012: Pope Benedict XVI sends his first tweet using the official (and newly created) papal account (@Pontifex), which now has 9.49 million followers and is used by Pope Francis.
- October 2013: Twitter updates its timeline by allowing photos and videos to be previewed in a tweet.
- November 2013: Twitter files its IPO (initial public offering), trading under the stock ticker TWTR.
- January 2015: Twitter launches group Direct Messages and mobile video.
- March 2015: Twitter announces the acquisition of Periscope,[29] a new app that lets you share and experience live video from your mobile phone.
- May 2015: Twitter teams with Google to bring relevant tweets to Google search results.

Twitter has revolutionized the way we communicate online in a number of ways—the most obvious of which being the 140-character limit per tweet.[30]

Additionally, Twitter introduced a new jargon, whose understanding is key to fully enjoying the platform. Here are some of the main Twitter terms that you need to know, in alphabetical order [17]:

- @: the @ sign is used to call out usernames in Tweets: "I 'm going to see @katyperry in concert tonight!". People will use your @username to mention you in Tweets, send you a message or link to your profile.
- **block**: once you block a Twitter user, that account will be unable to follow you or add you to their Twitter lists, and you will not receive a notification if they mention you in a Tweet.
- **Direct Messages**: private messages sent from one Twitter user to another Twitter user. You can use Direct Messages for one-on-one private conversations, or between groups of users.

---

[29]https://www.periscope.tv/.

[30]There are many guidelines on how to write effectively in 140 characters or less on the Web, such as [7].

- **follow** (verb): Twitter's term for subscribing to another Twitter account. Anyone on Twitter can follow or unfollow anyone else at any time, with the exception of blocked accounts.
- **follow(s)** (noun): the result of someone following your Twitter account. You can see your *follow count*, that is, how many follows (or followers) you have, from your Twitter profile.
- **follower**: another Twitter user who has followed you to receive your Tweets in their Home stream.
- **hashtag**: any word or phrase immediately preceded by the # symbol. When you click on a hashtag, you'll see other Tweets containing the same keyword or topic.
- **like** (noun): liking a Tweet indicates that you appreciate it. You can find all of your likes by clicking the likes tab on your profile.
- **like** (verb): when you tap the heart icon, you indicate that you like a Tweet and the author will see that you appreciate it.
- **list**: you can create a group list of other Twitter users by topic or interest or social circle (for example, a list of friends, coworkers, celebrities, athletes). Twitter lists also contain a timeline of Tweets from the specific users that were added to the list, offering you a way to follow individual accounts as a group on Twitter.
- **mention**: the act of mentioning other users in your Tweet by including the @ sign followed directly by their username is called a mention. The expression also refers to Tweets in which your @username was included.
- **protected Tweets**: Tweets are public by default. Choosing to protect your Tweets means that your Tweets will only be seen by your followers.
- **reply**: a response to another user's Tweet that begins with the @username of the person you're replying to. Replies to public tweets are also public.
- **Retweet (or simply RT)** (noun): a Tweet that you forward to your followers. RTs are often used to pass along news or other valuable discoveries on Twitter. Retweets always retain their original attribution.
- **Retweet** (verb): the act of sharing another user's Tweet to all of your followers by clicking on the Retweet button.
- **timeline**: a real-time stream of Tweets. Your Home stream, for instance, is where you see all the Tweets shared by your friends and other people you follow.
- **trends**: a Trend is a topic or hashtag determined algorithmically to be one of the most popular on Twitter at that moment. You can choose to tailor Trends based on your location and who you follow.
- **Tweet** (noun): a Tweet may contain photos, videos, links and up to 140 characters of text. Tweets get shown in Twitter timelines or are embedded in websites and blogs.
- **Tweet** (verb): the act of sending a Tweet.
- **who to follow**: an automated list of recommended accounts we think you might find interesting, based on the types of accounts you already follow and who those people follow.

4.4   Concluding Remarks

Due to their constant presence in our lives, social networks have had a markedly strong social impact. The lines between offline and virtual life have been forever blurred. Moreover, the concept of digital identity and online social interactions have become the topics of many discussions [3].

Most of such discussions are better left to experts in social sciences, but a fundamental question remains: **To share or not to share** (images, updates, current emotional state, innermost thoughts, current location, etc. with friends/followers in social networks)? This question can be broken down into six subquestions, as follows:

- **Why?**
  Determining the *motive* for sharing an item should be the first step.
- **What?**
  Establishing the *nature of the content* that you are about to share is another important checkpoint. For example, if it is a highly personal item but you want to record it for posterity, writing it on a journaling app might be more appropriate than sharing it on a social network.
- **How much?**
  We live in an age of reduced attention span and TMI (too much information). Posting updates with excessive *amount of detail* may hurt you twice: some will not invest the time to read it through the end, others may start tuning out to your posts because there are just too many of them.
- **How often?**
  Adjusting the *frequency* (and timing) of your updates is such an important skill that there are many apps and services to assist you in picking the right days and times of the week to post on your Facebook page, Twitter feed, or Instagram account.
- **With whom?**
  You must know your *audience*. If you have many diverse interests, consider segmenting your audience, so that your message will reach those who might be interested in it; not more, not less.
- **Using which app or social network?**
  The *method* by which you share should be appropriate to the item being shared (e.g., photos on Instagram, short text snippets on Twitter, longer posts on Facebook), but the borders have blurred and it's very easy (and tempting) to "also share" on other social media apps an item originally posted in one of them.

To conclude this section, these are some simple (and general) recommendations on the issue of sharing:

- Distinguish *public* from *private*.
  Many embarrassing situations in social networks arise from poor understanding of which updates, posts, or replies are public, and which ones are private. Learn what is private or public in a specific platform (Facebook, Twitter) *before* starting posting content.

Moreover, keep in mind these important rules of thumb:

1. Assume that anything you post on any social network is "potentially public". After all, even you use direct messaging or restrict the audience of your posts, once the content is "out there" you cannot control what the recipients will do with it.
2. Once you post something online, it will potentially live forever. Think of how many controversial tweets from celebrities and politicians (which were eventually deleted) make for headlines in news outlets on a regular basis.

- Build groups or lists (if possible).

  Not every post or update will be equally interesting to all of your friends/followers. Segmenting your audience into groups may give you a better way to communicate with a specific subset of people on topics that they care about. It is a win-win situation: on one hand you don't refrain from posting something because maybe a few followers would not like it; on the other hand, your followers will be spared from updates on topics that you care about but they don't. This can be done trough the use of lists in Facebook and—in a similar vein—using multiple accounts on Twitter.

- Know your audience.

  Who are your friends/followers? Why do they follow your updates? What is it about the content, style, frequency, and tone of your posts that makes them worth reading, forwarding (re-tweeting or sharing), or being "liked" (or marked as favorite)? You should be able to monitor the reactions to your posts[31] and adjust subsequent updates accordingly.

- Understand your medium.

  Each social network is different and so are the usage patterns, skills, and expectations of its users. For example, in highly visual social media apps (such as Instagram), the visual quality of your photos will be a primary factor in building an audience and getting attention,[32] whereas in a fast-paced social network such as Twitter, timing is of utmost importance.

- Have fun!

  Despite all their drawbacks, social networks can be an amazing way to make new friends and keep in touch with existing ones; learn new topics; discover new places, books, people, institutions; give and receive help and encouragement; receive feedback on ideas; and engage with many individuals and companies that would be completely out of your reach before. Enjoy the opportunity and make the best of what social networks have to offer!

---

[31]For individual users with a few hundred friends or followers, this can be done "manually" by looking at which posts received more feedback, for example. For social media accounts with larger number of followers—companies, celebrities, politicians—there are many analytics tools to measure one's impact (for example, Klout [8]) and/or assist in such tasks.

[32]Knowing how to use strategic hashtags will also help tremendously in attracting followers that might not know you otherwise.

Takeaways from this chapter:

- Social networks have impacted work, politics, communications patterns, as well as the way people consume and share information about virtually every topic.
- Social networks can be established at multiple levels and for different purposes, such as: professional connections and opportunities, image and video sharing, location sharing through "checkins", or real-time rich messaging.
- 65 % of American adults use social networking sites. Worldwide, there are 2.04 billion social network users, a number expected to grow to 2.55 billion in 2018.
- Facebook is the largest and most popular social network platform in use today, with more than 1.5 billion users worldwide.
- There are very good reasons to (not) be on Facebook, including social pressure and privacy concerns.
- Social network users are expected to follow proper etiquette. However, since the medium is rather new, there are many cases where this does not happen.
- Twitter is an online social networking service that enables users to send short 140-character messages called *tweets*.
- Twitter has become incredibly popular among newscasters, politician, movie and music stars, professional athletes, and other celebrities.
- Twitter usage during events (*live-tweeting*) has become a popular way for users to engage online with others while sharing their thoughts on a current event, for example a TV series season finale.
- Twitter helped popularize the notion and usage of hashtags.
- Before (over)sharing items, opinions, photos, or personal events on social networks, one should reflect upon whether there is a good reason for doing so and whether it will reach the right audience.

References

1. Facebook 350 million photos each day - business insider. http://www.businessinsider.com/facebook-350-million-photos-each-day-2013-9. Accessed 24 June 2016
2. Facebook: mobile-only users 2016 — statistic. http://www.statista.com/statistics/281600/number-of-mobile-only-facebook-users/. Accessed 25 June 2016
3. Global social media ranking 2016 — statistic. http://www.statista.com/statistics/272014/global-social-networks-ranked-by-number-of-users/. Accessed 25 June 2016
4. Global social media ranking 2016 — statistic. http://www.statista.com/statistics/272014/global-social-networks-ranked-by-number-of-users/. Accessed 29 June 2016
5. History of Facebook: all the major updates and changes from 2004–2016 — Know your mobile. http://www.knowyourmobile.com/apps/facebook/21807/history-facebook-all-major-updates-changes-2004-2016. Accessed 25 June 2016

6. History of Facebook on a timeline. http://www.startlin.es/timelines/facebook/. Accessed 25 June 2016
7. How to write in 140 characters or less. http://www.lifehack.org/articles/communication/how-to-write-in-140-characters-or-less.html. Accessed 29 June 2016
8. Klout — Be known for what you love. https://klout.com/home. Accessed 27 June 2016
9. List of defunct social networking websites - wikipedia, the free encyclopedia. https://en.wikipedia.org/wiki/List_of_defunct_social_networking_websites. Accessed 25 June 2016
10. List of social networking websites - wikipedia, the free encyclopedia. https://en.wikipedia.org/wiki/List_of_social_networking_websites. Accessed 25 June 2016
11. Milestones — About. https://about.twitter.com/company/press/milestones. Accessed 29 June 2016
12. Number of worldwide social network users 2010–2019 — statistic. http://www.statista.com/statistics/278414/number-of-worldwide-social-network-users/. Accessed 25 June 2016
13. Pew Research Center (2015) Social media usage: 2005–2015. http://www.pewinternet.org/2015/10/08/social-networking-usage-2005-2015/
14. Social media and events - statistics and facts — Statista. http://www.statista.com/topics/2040/social-media-and-events/. Accessed 29 June 2016
15. Social networks - statistics and facts — statista. http://www.statista.com/topics/1164/social-networks/. Accessed 25 June 2016
16. Taigman Y, Yang M, Ranzato M, Wolf L (2014) Deepface: closing the gap to human-level performance in face verification. In Proceedings of the IEEE conference on computer vision and pattern recognition, pp 1701–1708
17. The twitter glossary — Twitter help center. https://support.twitter.com/articles/166337. Accessed 29 June 2016
18. Timeline: key dates in Facebook's 10-year history - Washington times. http://www.washingtontimes.com/news/2014/feb/4/timeline-key-dates-in-facebooks-10-year-history/. Accessed 25 June 2016
19. Timeline of twitter's history - The Washington post. https://apps.washingtonpost.com/g/page/business/timeline-of-twitters-history/570/. Accessed 29 June 2016
20. Twitter - statistics and facts — Statista. http://www.statista.com/topics/737/twitter/. Accessed 27 June 2016
21. Twitter: most-followed accounts worldwide 2016 — Statistic. http://www.statista.com/statistics/273172/twitter-accounts-with-the-most-followers-worldwide/. Accessed 29 June 2016
22. Urban dictionary: vaguebooking. https://www.urbandictionary.com/define.php?term=Vaguebooking. Accessed 29 June 2016

Chapter 5
Image and Video Everywhere!

Abstract During the past decade, there have been substantial technological advances in the ways we capture, produce, edit, share, remix, and distribute images and videos. In parallel with more sophisticated gadgets and apps, our habits have also changed, from the way we watch TV to the number of images we produce, consume, and share every day. This chapter focuses on apps, gadgets, websites, and social networks whose primary emphasis is on *visual information*. We present a selected set of apps and techniques used to capture, produce, edit, share, remix, and distribute images and videos. We also discuss some of the technical challenges behind the tasks of organizing, annotating, and finding relevant images and videos.

5.1 Introduction

The tremendous importance of rich visual information in our daily lives can be attested by the popularity of social networks, the ever-growing use of video as a medium, and the compelling graphics and visual effects in movies and games. We live in a world where images and videos are, indeed, everywhere [16]! Recent statistics indicate that more than 1.7 billion people have a smartphone with camera [25], at least 350 million photos are uploaded to Facebook every day [7], and Snapchat, Instagram, Facebook and WhatsApp users (combined) share at least 1.8 billion photos each day [38].

5.2 How to Use Images and Videos Today

Thanks to technological developments during the past 25 years, there has been a significant increase in the production and consumption of visually rich contents, including high-quality images and high-definition videos.

There is, however, a big mismatch between the processes of *producing* visual resources and *organizing* them for further cataloguing and consumption. Production tasks (such as capturing, producing, editing, sharing, remixing, and distributing visual content) have become easier thanks to an extensive array of highly-capable

O. Marques, *Innovative Technologies in Everyday Life*, SpringerBriefs
in Computer Science, DOI 10.1007/978-3-319-45699-7_5

devices and powerful apps. Organizational tasks (such as annotating, tagging, searching for and retrieving visual content), however, remain difficult and expensive.

5.2.1   Taking Pictures and Videos

Taking pictures and videos has become an easy and inexpensive task. If you are reading this book, you probably have a camera (app) with you, embedded in your smartphone. In fact, I can almost bet that you do not see the need for carrying an *actual* camera around, except for special occasions. After all, the resolution and quality of images and videos produced with a smartphone camera are appropriate for everyday needs and even acceptable for venturing into amateur photography. Moreover, the convenience of having a lightweight device that is always available often trumps the desire for a better equipment setup. This has not stopped the opportunity for a new market segment (namely, accessories for iPhone and Android photography) to develop.

The popularization of using smartphone cameras can be attested by the birth of a new term: iPhoneography, defined as—you guessed it!—"the art of shooting and processing photos with an Apple iPhone." As a measure of success of the new field, one of the many books in this space, Roberts's *The Art of iPhoneography: A Guide to Mobile Creativity* [23], now in its second edition, has sold tens of thousands of copies and is available in a dozen languages.

One of the most notable cultural phenomena of our times—driven, in part, by the availability of a camera at all times—is the *selfie*, which was selected as the Oxford Dictionary's new word of the year in 2013, and defined as: "A photograph that one has taken of oneself, typically one taken with a smartphone or webcam and shared via social media." As a humorous example of the many selfie-related discussions and incidents, a recent article on The Telegraph compiled "the most irritating selfies of all time", a list topped by "Beyoncé in the Louvre" that also includes "Anything with Kim Kardashian", "Selfies with endangered animals", "Disaster selfies", and "Fan meets celebrity selfies" [31].

As a poignant example of this tectonic shift from an analog world—where film-based photography was the norm—to the current digital photography era, we should mention the demise of Kodak (1888–2012), a company responsible for bringing the first simple camera to the market, which had at some point in time (1996, to be more precise) been considered the fifth most valuable brand in the world, worth (at that time) \$31 billion, and whose name had been associated with photography for several generations.

5.2.2 Editing Pictures and Videos

It has never been easier to enhance and fix a photo or perform basic video editing (such as trimming) and today's smartphones provide built-in features for such tasks. If the functionality provided by your smartphone's operating system and built-in apps is note enough, there is plenty of options to choose from: it is estimated that 2.29 % [5] of the two million apps available at the Apple App store [4] belong to the *Photo and Video* category, which translates to more than 45 thousand apps to chose from—for the iOS alone!

In fact, there is even an app about (photography) apps, AppAlchemy, "a 100 page interactive iPad eBook on experimental photography processes with iPhone apps" [3], created by Dan Marcolina, which features overviews of essential apps, step-by-step video tutorials, and many links and examples of work based around each highlighted app.

Outside of the smartphone app ecosystem, there are numerous options for image and video editing for different operating systems as well as attractive alternatives for photoshopping[1] in your browser (see [30] for suggestions) or doing video editing entirely online (see [34] for a recently compiled list).

5.2.3 Storing Pictures and Videos

Digital images and videos often occupy large amounts of disk space, which has led to the development of compression standards (such as JPEG and MPEG) whose original goal was to reduce the size of image and video files for storage and transmission purposes. Interestingly enough, since the early 1990s, as compressed digital image and video standards evolved, other parallel developments took place: on one hand, storage media became significantly cheaper and broadband Internet access at higher speeds became the norm in most developed countries; on the other hand, we started producing more visual content, of higher resolution, and becoming used to consuming such contents in high-quality devices.

There are many (inexpensive) alternatives to storing images and videos today, from lightweight portable devices (SD cards, CDs, DVDs, Flash (USB) drives, etc.) to cloud-based storage solutions which can offer storage quotas as generous as Flickr's 1 TB (roughly two million high-res images or 800 h of HD videos) per user, for free. As an additional benefit, cloud-based storage allows you to access your visual assets virtually from everywhere using a variety of devices.

---

[1]Photoshop—transitive verb: to alter (a digital image) with Photoshop software or other image-editing software especially in a way that distorts reality (as for deliberately deceptive purposes) [19].

5.2.4 Publishing, Tagging and Sharing Pictures and Videos

There are tens of websites for photo hosting and sharing to choose from. Some of the most popular, and best reviewed, examples are [8]:

- **Flickr**[2]: Flickr was the first well-known image sharing site targeted at photographers and photo lovers. It has experienced many significant changes over the past few years, but it is still an excellent great place to host your photos, thanks to its popularity with a large community of photographers, the option to make your photos public or private at any time, multiple licensing options (including Creative Commons), and groups for just about every possible interest. Perhaps best of all, Flickr is free (all you need is a Yahoo account) for an ad-supported account with 1TB of storage (limited to 200 MB per photo and 1 GB per video, with a maximum 3-min duration) [8].
- **Google Photos**[3]: Google Photos (formerly Picasa Web Albums[4]) is another excellent free[5] alternative for hosting, managing, organizing, and sharing your photos, especially if you already use other Google products, apps, and services. It has a vast array of useful tools and features, such as: the option to automatically upload photos and videos from your Android or iOS device, as well as back up and store your photos from multiple sources; powerful Web-based image editing tools; and easy and clever ways of organizing photos based on "people", "places", "things" (and more) [8]. One of its coolest new features is the *Assistant*,[6] which (automatically) creates collages, movies, animations, and even suggests filters for your photos or stitch them to form a panorama!
- **Smugmug**[7]: Smugmug has been around since 2002 and continues to offer tools and services for photographers to showcase their full resolution photos and videos while simultaneously fostering a great sense of community among its users. Smugmug also gives photographers complete control over licensing, download options, watermarking, and more. Smugmug is a paid service, with plans that range from $40 to $300 per year, depending on the amount of storage, customization options, and other aspects [8].
- **imgur**[8]: Imgur is famously known (especially among the young, social media savvy, Reddit[9] users) as an image sharing site designed for quick, disposable image sharing and focused on viral images, memes, and GIFs. It is not an image

---

[2]http://www.flickr.com/.

[3]http://photos.google.com/.

[4]http://picasaweb.google.com.

[5]Your storage space is shared with Google Drive, and therefore limited to how much Google Drive space you might have available [8].

[6]http://photos.google.com/assistant.

[7]http://www.smugmug.com/.

[8]http://imgur.com/.

[9]http://www.reddit.com/.

hosting site in the classic sense, with beautiful galleries and attention to photo rights, credits, licensing, and presentation, but it is fast, easy to use, and has a huge user base behind it [8].

- **500px**[10]: 500px is a social network for photographers and distinguishes itself from other image sharing and hosting sites by calling itself a place to share your best work, to showcase your photography, and to get involved with other people who have the same eye for photos or passion for visual arts. Users there have their own profiles, with their own galleries and photos proudly displayed under their names, can follow other photographers, and photographers get control over licensing and usage of their photos. 500px is also an excellent source of desktop wallpapers, as well as a great photo browser and slideshow creator for iPad or Android [8].
- **Dropbox**[11]: Dropbox is a file-sharing service that has also entered the photo and video hosting and sharing space after their introduction of the *Automatic backup* option, which can be enabled to allow automatic uploads from your device's camera roll to Dropbox. Once uploaded to Dropbox, it is easy to create albums and organize photos by date.
- **Amazon Prime Photos**[12]: Amazon Prime Photos is a convenient free[13] alternative to Amazon Prime[14] members, due to the fact that it easily syncs and automatically backs up photos from your phone or your desktop to Amazon's Cloud Drive [8].

On the video arena, YouTube is—by far—the larger and most popular website for hosting user-generated videos, with more than one billion monthly users [28], eight times larger than one of its closest competitors, Vimeo [35].

When it comes to sharing photos (and short videos), Facebook (Sect. 4.2), Instagram (Sect. 5.3.1), and Snapchat (Sect. 5.3.3) are the leading apps—combined, they have more than two billion monthly active users.

5.2.5 Searching and Retrieving Pictures and Videos

Despite many technological advances in the field of Visual Information Retrieval (VIR) [16], the tasks of searching and retrieving relevant and useful images and videos remains rather challenging, whether we are searching for photos and videos

---

[10]http://500px.com/.

[11]http://www.dropbox.com/.

[12]http://www.amazon.com/clouddrive/primephotos.

[13]Amazon Prime members have unlimited free storage of photos. There is, however, a very modest limit on video (or "other files") storage: only 5 GB. If you want additional storage space for videos, it will cost you $59.99 per year.

[14]https://goo.gl/qope7j.

from our personal computer or the Web at large. We wish today's search engines were capable of being presented with an image or video clip and answering questions such as: "Which animal is this?", "How much does this product cost?", "Who painted this work of art?", "Who is this player?" or "Can you find me more images or videos like this?" Alas, the future is not yet here, at least not in this field of research.

There are, however, several commercial apps and websites for visual information retrieval worth paying attention to. Examples of content-based visual search websites include: the *search by image* option in Google image search,[15] the *image match* option within Bing image search,[16] and TinEye.[17] In the *Mobile Visual Search (MVS)* [10] category, CamFind[18] is allegedly the best example of a mature, robust, versatile, and well-rounded MVS app [16].

There is also a growing number of examples in which the ability to perform visual searches is embedded into an app. Examples include [16].:

- Vivino[19] and Next Glass[20]—apps for wine and beer enthusiasts which allows users to take a photo of a wine or beer label and instantly learn additional information about that wine (or beer), such as: rating, reviews, nutritional information, and average price.
- The Amazon mobile app,[21] which has a visual search option that is remarkably fast and accurate and works in real-time—i.e. without requiring that the user first takes a picture and then presses the search button—which is also available as a separate app, Flow.[22]
- The Pinterest Visual Search Tool,[23] which gives users the ability to zoom within a particular image and drag the zoom tool over the specific region of interest in the Pin and search for it; visually similar results appear almost instantly and integrate well with the app's user interface. Additionally, users can refine the results by filtering with a specific tag.

---

[15]http://images.google.com/.

[16]http://www.bing.com/images.

[17]http://www.tineye.com/.

[18]http://camfindapp.com/.

[19]http://www.vivino.com/.

[20]http://nextglass.co/.

[21]http://www.amazon.com/gp/feature.html?docId=1000625601.

[22]http://flow.a9.com/.

[23]http://blog.pinterest.com/en/our-crazy-fun-new-visual-search-tool.

5.3 Image Sharing Apps

5.3.1 Instagram

Instagram is a social networking service and app for sharing photos.[24] In its 6 years of existence, Instagram has experienced exponential growth in its user base and has become a household name for photo sharing and social media buzz. Launched in October 2010, it reached one million users in less than 3 months, ten million users in less than a year, was recognized by Apple as the "iPhone App of the Year" at the end of 2011 (months before its Android app was released), was sold to Facebook for $1 billion USD in 2012, and has now more than 500 million users (as of June 2016) [14]. In the United States, the current Instagram penetration rate among internet users is 28 % and the number of Instagram users is projected to surpass 106 million users in 2018 [12].

Instagram makes it easy for its users to also share their content on a variety of social networks such as Facebook, Twitter, Flickr and Tumblr [12]. Many users follow celebrities on Instagram to gain a glimpse into their glamorous lives, following a similar usage pattern to Twitter [12]. As of June 2016, the most-followed celebrities on Instagram include Selena Gomez, Taylor Swift, Kim Kardashian, Ariana Grande, Justin Bieber, Beyonce, and soccer superstar Cristiano Ronaldo [15], each of them with 50 million followers or more. Instagram also shows big potential in the area of social media marketing and social commerce, especially for visually rich items such as luxury and fashion products: 65 % of leading brands already have an active Instagram account—but only 19 % of those brands have more than 100,000 followers [12].

The vast majority (98 % [36]) of Instagram users interact with the service via the mobile app, which basically allows its users to take pictures, edit them with a selection of digital filters, add descriptive text (including hashtags), and share with their followers. Instagram filters (Fig. 5.1) were part of the initial appeal of the app and have been intrinsically related to its success and have become a major topic of interest.[25]

The Instagram "ecosystem" includes many apps and services, covering a wide range of aspects, such as: taking better pictures and videos, applying rich visual effects to your photos before sharing on Instagram, and printing your favorite photos. Professional Instagram users might also want to consider using a business analytics and marketing service, such as Iconosquare.[26]

---

[24] As of June 2013, Instagram also started to offer video sharing.

[25] See [29] for a recent study on the most popular Instagram filters around the world, [13] for the stories behind the *names* of several Instagram filters, and [22] for a story on a surprising recent trend: naming babies after Instagram filters!

[26] http://iconosquare.com/.

Fig. 5.1 Examples of Instagram filters available in 2011 (*source*: Wikimedia Commons)

5.3.2   *Pinterest*

Pinterest is a Web-based service for visual discovery, collection, sharing, and storage. Pinterest users can create and share their collections of visual bookmarks (which are called *boards*) by selecting an item, page, website, or photo and *pinning* it to an existing or newly created board. Users save and share pins from multiple resources onto boards based on different criteria, such as similar characteristics, a theme, or a project, for example: birthday parties, planning a vacation, writing a book, interior decorating, holidays.

Content of interest can be pinned to a Pinterest board through an increasingly popular red-and-white "Pin It" button, which is available as a browser button[27] or as a part of the "social media sharing" toolbar of many websites and blogs.

Pinterest was founded in 2010 and was the fastest site in history to reach (in early 2012) ten million unique monthly visitors [21]. Its current user base is estimated to be more than 100 million monthly active *Pinners* [1], 56 % of which are women [20].

5.3.3   *Snapchat*

Snapchat is a mobile photo and video sharing app that allows the creation of multimedia messages, referred to as *snaps*, which can consist of a photo or a short video, and can be edited with text, filters, stickers or other overlays. Snaps can be

---

[27]http://about.pinterest.com/en/browser-button.

shared as a semi-public *story*, which is automatically shared with the user's contact list, or sent privately [26].

Snapchat was initially launched (in 2011) as a way to share pictures via private message *snaps* that could be viewed only for a user-specified length of time before becoming inaccessible [26]. True to its original intent, all contents on Snapchat are of temporary nature. Stories, for example, are accessible for 24 h.

Snapchat is one of the fastest growing social apps and networks worldwide. It is particularly popular among teenagers and young adults in the United States, which have made Snapchat their most used social media site, with a 72 % reach—ahead of Facebook (68 %) and Instagram (66 %), with Twitter (36 %) in a distant fourth place [17].

Snapchat stories are created by at least one-third of its 100 million daily active users worldwide [26], generating an enormous amount of visual content: as of February 2016, Snapchat users are watching ten billion mobile videos a day on the application [27].

A significant number of Snapchat users are willing to use the app to pay for online and mobile content, with music downloads and TV and movie streaming being the most popular types of paid content. The platform has become a popular vehicle for visually strong brands—such as sportswear, beauty and fashion—to reach teens and Millennials [26].

5.4 The Video (R)evolution

There have been substantial changes in TV watching habits during the past 15 years, since the first generation digital video recorders (DVRs) arrived at the American market, led by TiVo,[28] which would eventually become a verb, defined in the Merriam-Webster dictionary as "to record (as a television program) with a DVR" [33]. We discovered that live television could be paused, commercials skipped, and favorite programs recorded automatically and made accessible using friendly menus. The arrival of DVRs—in parallel with other developments, such as the DVD—effectively rendered VCRs obsolete.

During the same timeframe, just about every aspect of TV, movie, and video production and consumption has changed dramatically. Here are a few examples of relatively recent (including a few short-lived) changes and advances in this area:

- TV sets become thinner, lighter, smarter, and the image resolution went from standard definition (SDTV, 525 horizontal lines) to high-definition (HDTV, 1080 lines), to ultra-high-definition (4K Ultra HD, 2160 lines).

---

[28]http://www.tivo.com/.

- The movie industry continues to struggle with shrinking revenues, closing theaters (despite a complete revamping of the distribution and projection infrastructure to implement the *digital cinema* vision), and the popularization of movies in 3D.
- We moved from renting DVDs from a physical Blockbuster store to having them delivered in the mail via Netflix[29] (and slowly replaced by Blu-Ray disks), to a world where there are many competing high-quality video streaming services to choose from—such as Netflix, Sling,[30] Amazon Instant Video,[31] and Hulu.[32]
- High-quality video contents (including movies and live TV) became available in a huge variety of devices, including: smart TVs, conventional set-top boxes (often with DVR capabilities), streaming media players (such as Roku,[33] Amazon Fire,[34] and Apple TV,[35]) game consoles (such as XBox,[36] PlayStation,[37] or Wii[38]), Blu-ray players, PCs, laptops, tablets, and—with great success and popularity—smartphones.
- Cable and satellite TV subscriptions have been partially replaced by services that use the Internet to deliver live TV (including premium channels, such as HBO Now[39]) in an increasingly popular movement known as "cord cutting" [32].
- Video on the Web become much more popular, faster, and less dependent on plugins, thanks to the evolution of technical standards such as HTML5 [11] and MPEG-DASH [18]. As a result, the once popular (and almost omnipresent) Flash Player is virtually dead [6].
- TV viewing habits have shifted dramatically. We have witnessed the birth of the "binge watching" mode (for TV series whose episodes are made available all at once, such as the ones produced by Netflix and Amazon), become used to "nonlinear video watching" [2], and increasingly more accustomed to a "second-screen experience" [24], for example to follow the "live tweeting" action of the stars of a TV show while the show is being broadcast for the first time.
- Today, we can easily shoot, edit, share and broadcast high-quality video using a smartphone, Internet connection, and a free hosting or streaming service, such as YouTube (Sect. 5.5) or Facebook Live.[40]

---

[29]http://www.netflix.com/.

[30]http://www.sling.com/.

[31]http://www.amazon.com/gp/video/getstarted/.

[32]http://www.hulu.com/.

[33]http://www.roku.com/.

[34]https://goo.gl/Fc8sYz.

[35]http://www.apple.com/tv/.

[36]http://www.xbox.com/.

[37]http://www.playstation.com.

[38]http://wii.com/.

[39]http://www.hbonow.com/.

[40]http://live.fb.com/about/.

5.5   YouTube

YouTube is a video-sharing website featuring an ever-growing[41] collection of user-generated and corporate media contents, including music videos, TV clips, video blogs, beauty and fashion tips, short original videos, as well as instructional videos and educational content (see Sect. 2.5.1) [39].

The platform, which was created in 2005 (and acquired by Google for $1.65 billion USD in late 2006), has slowly become one of the most visited websites in the world and a global phenomenon. During its less than 12 years of existence, YouTube has become a synonym for "online video platform", with impressive usage statistics, such as:

- Reach: in the first quarter of 2015, more than 80 % of global internet users had visited YouTube in the last month [39].
- Popularity: In the United States, it is the second largest social media website after Facebook, accounting for over 22 % of social media traffic [37].
- Mobility: As of mid 2015, approximately half of U.S. mobile users accessed YouTube via a mobile device (smartphone or tablet) [39].

Originally conceived as a platform on which users could post original content that they thought to be interesting, funny or somehow worth sharing, YouTube has since become a powerful money-making tool. YouTube generates the majority of its revenues through in-site advertising, with owners of popular channels being eligible to receive a percentage of the revenue they helped create [39]. Some of the most popular YouTube channels[42] are maintained by traditional brands, while many others are led by emerging online personalities. One of the most famous YouTube stars is video game commentator PewDiePie, the screen name for Swedish 26-year-old Felix Kjellberg, whose YouTube channel (as of June 2016) has more than 45 million subscribers, and whose videos have been seen more than 12.527 billion times. PewDiePie appeared at the top of Forbes' October 2015 list of the richest YouTube stars with a reported $12 million USD earned in 2015 [9].

YouTube has recently expanded its offerings with the introduction of YouTube Red,[43] a premium subscription service that offers uninterrupted music, advertising-free streaming of all videos, offline capabilities, as well as access to exclusive original content.

---

[41] As of July 2015, more than 400 h of video content were uploaded to YouTube every minute [39].
[42] See http://vidstatsx.com/ for very detailed up-to-date statistics on YouTube channels.
[43] http://www.youtube.com/red.

5.6   Concluding Remarks

This chapter provided a very broad and brief overview of a subset of apps, services, websites, devices and technologies associated with the creation, editing, and publishing of visual information. This is a wonderfully rich field, with exciting new developments—such as: virtual reality (VR) sets, wearable cameras, 360° video, and much more—happening at ultrafast speed, making yesterday's greatest product or service become today's mainstream and tomorrow's museum piece.

Takeaways from this chapter:

- In today's developed world, images and videos everywhere; visual content is being created, uploaded, shared, and watched at astonishing rates.
- There is a big mismatch between the processes of *producing* visual resources and *organizing* them for further cataloguing and consumption. Important tasks—such as annotating, tagging, searching for and retrieving visual content—remain difficult and expensive.
- Choosing the best apps for handling visual information can be a very difficult task: there are more than 45,000 apps in the *Photo & video* category of the iOS App Store alone.
- Facebook, Instagram, and—more recently—Snapchat are the leading apps for sharing images and videos with friends or followers. Combined, they have more than two billion monthly active users.
- During the past decade, just about every aspect of TV, movie, and video production and consumption has changed dramatically.
- YouTube has become the de facto online video platform, with more than 400 h of video content uploaded to its servers every minute.
- Leading YouTube channels have tens of millions of subscribers and provide a very lucrative platform for their creators.

References

1. 100 million of the most interesting people we know — pinterest blog. https://blog.pinterest.com/en/100-million-most-interesting-people-we-know. Accessed 26 June 2016
2. 2015: A video space odyssey – value shifts in the tv and video ecosystem. http://www.strategyand.pwc.com/reports/2015-video-space-odyssey-value. Accessed 26 June 2016
3. Appalchemy on the app store. https://itunes.apple.com/us/app/appalchemy/id560801711?mt=8. Accessed 24 June 2016
4. Apple app store: number of available apps 2016 — statistic. http://www.statista.com/statistics/263795/number-of-available-apps-in-the-apple-app-store/. Accessed 24 June 2016
5. Apple: most popular app store categories 2016 — statistic. http://www.statista.com/statistics/270291/popular-categories-in-the-app-store/. Accessed 24 June 2016

6. Chart: Bye bye flash! — Statista. https://www.statista.com/chart/3796/websites-using-flash/. Accessed 28 June 2016
7. Facebook 350 million photos each day - business insider. http://www.businessinsider.com/facebook-350-million-photos-each-day-2013-9. Accessed 24 June 2016
8. Five best image hosting web sites. http://lifehacker.com/5808625/five-best-web-sites-for-image-hosting-and-photo-sharing/. Accessed 24 June 2016
9. Forbes lists video gamer 'PewDiePie' as top YouTube earner — Technology news — US News. http://www.usnews.com/news/business/articles/2015/10/15/forbes-lists-video-gamer-pewdiepie-as-top-youtube-earner. Accessed 28 June 2016
10. Girod B, Chandrasekhar V, Chen DM, Cheung N-M, Grzeszczuk R, Reznik Y, Takacs G, Tsai SS, Vedantham R (2011) Mobile visual search. IEEE Signal Process Mag 28(4):61–76
11. HTML5. https://www.w3.org/TR/html5/. Accessed 28 June 2016
12. Instagram - statistics and facts — statista. http://www.statista.com/topics/1882/instagram/. Accessed 26 June 2016
13. Instagram filters names meanings. http://goo.gl/eyJGtV. Accessed 26 June 2016
14. Instagram monthly active users 2016 — statistic. http://www.statista.com/statistics/253577/number-of-monthly-active-instagram-users/. Accessed 26 June 2016
15. Instagram: most-followed accounts worldwide 2016 — statistic. http://www.statista.com/statistics/421169/most-followers-instagram/. Accessed 26 June 2016
16. Marques O (2016) Visual information retrieval: the state of the art. IT Prof 18(4):7–9
17. Most popular social media with U.S. teens 2016 — Statistic. http://www.statista.com/statistics/199242/social-media-and-networking-sites-used-by-us-teenagers/. Accessed 28 June 2016
18. MPEG-DASH — MPEG. http://mpeg.chiariglione.org/standards/mpeg-dash. 06/28/2016 Accessed 28 June 2016
19. Photoshop — definition of photoshop by Merriam-Webster. http://www.merriam-webster.com/dictionary/photoshop. Accessed 24 June 2016
20. Pinterest: gender distribution of global audiences 2014 — statistic. http://www.statista.com/statistics/328095/pinterest-global-gender/. Accessed 26 June 2016
21. Pinterest hits 10 million U.S. monthly uniques faster than any standalone site ever -comscore — techcrunch. https://techcrunch.com/2012/02/07/pinterest-monthly-uniques/. Accessed 26 June 2016
22. Popular baby names 2015 instagram. http://www.refinery29.com/2015/12/98587/popular-baby-names-instagram. Accessed 26 June 2016
23. Roberts S (2012) The art of iphoneography: a guide to mobile creativity. Pixiq, Asheville
24. Second screen usage - statistics and facts — Statista. http://www.statista.com/topics/2531/second-screen-usage/. Accessed 28 June 2016
25. Smartphone users worldwide will total 1.75 billion in 2014. http://www.emarketer.com/Article/Smartphone-Users-Worldwide-Will-Total-175-Billion-2014/1010536. Accessed 24 June 2016
26. Snapchat - statistics and facts — statista. http://www.statista.com/topics/2882/snapchat/. Accessed 26 June 2016
27. Snapchat user 'stories' fuel 10 billion daily video views - Bloomberg. http://www.bloomberg.com/news/articles/2016-04-28/snapchat-user-content-fuels-jump-to-10-billion-daily-video-views. Accessed 28 June 2016
28. Statistics - youtube. https://www.youtube.com/yt/press/statistics.html. Accessed 24 June 2016
29. Study: the most popular instagram filters from around the world – design school. https://designschool.canva.com/blog/popular-instagram-filters/. Accessed 26 June 2016
30. The 9 best browser-based photo editors available today. http://thenextweb.com/creativity/2014/02/24/9-browser-based-photo-editing-tools/. Accessed 24 June 2016
31. The Telegraph (2014) The most irritating selfies of all time. http://www.telegraph.co.uk/news/celebritynews/11159162/Beyonce-most-irritating-selfies-of-all-time.html
32. The ultimate cord cutter's guide — PCMag.com. http://goo.gl/QDTgTV. Accessed 28 June 2016

33. Tivo — Definition of Tivo by Merriam-Webster. http://www.merriam-webster.com/dictionary/TiVo. Accessed 28 June 2016
34. Top 10 best online video editors for video editing online. http://filmora.wondershare.com/video-editor/free-online-video-editor.html. Accessed 24 June 2016
35. Top 15 most popular video websites — June 2016. http://www.ebizmba.com/articles/video-websites. Accessed 24 June 2016
36. U.S. social media site usage by platform 2014 — statistic. http://www.statista.com/statistics/294445/minutes-spent-on-us-media-sites-by-platform/. Accessed 26 June 2016
37. U.S. top social media sites visit share 2016 — statistic. http://www.statista.com/statistics/265773/market-share-of-the-most-popular-social-media-websites-in-the-us/. Accessed 28 June 2016
38. We now upload and share over 1.8 billion photos each day: Meeker Internet report. http://tech.firstpost.com/news-analysis/now-upload-share-1-8-billion-photos-everyday-meeker-report-224688.html. Accessed 24 June 2016
39. YouTube - statistics and facts — Statista. http://www.statista.com/topics/2019/youtube/. Accessed 27 June 2016

Chapter 6
Conclusion

Abstract In this brief chapter I offer suggestions for reflections on how emerging technologies are changing our habits and what the future may hold. This chapter also offers practical tips on how to live in an "always-on, 24/7" world, without losing our minds in the process.

6.1 Three Challenges

As we approach the end of this guided tour of innovative technologies, I would like to offer a few suggestions for reflections on how they are changing our habits and what the future may hold. I believe we can agree that technology has impacted our lives for better in multiple directions. We can also agree, however, that the same technological advancements that have brought greater comfort, closer proximity with loved ones, and multiple engaging ways of learning new things, have also contributed to the dawn of an era where everyone seems to be "always-on, 24/7". Worse yet, those of us who are not operating within this mindset have started to feel the threat of being excluded from some of the exciting new developments in the world around us.

I see three main challenges associated with the impact of technology in modern life:

1. **Information overload**
   The amount of information available for immediate consumption today is greater than ever before and keeps growing exponentially. In addition to traditional sources (books, newspapers, magazines, journals, museums, encyclopedias), there is an increasing percentage of user-contributed content in almost every site, app, or platform. Moreover, much of this content is packaged in visually attractive ways and delivered with a sense of (often unwarranted) urgency. Deciding upon what to consume, how much, how frequently, and from which sources, is not an easy exercise.

   My recommendations in this regard are as follows: (1) Be selective in your choice of trusted sources and learn, over time, to discriminate the *signal* from the *noise*. (2) Do not allow others' sense of urgency or importance to have a

O. Marques, *Innovative Technologies in Everyday Life*, SpringerBriefs
in Computer Science, DOI 10.1007/978-3-319-45699-7_6

disproportional impact on your life. (3) Use tools (such as Evernote[1] or Pocket[2]) to keep a record of information that you want to keep and organize for later consumption. (4) Accept information overload as a fact of life—the days of reading the morning paper front to back and feeling informed about what was going on in the world, before heading out to work, are gone forever.

2. Technical complexity

Most of the gadgets, websites, and apps in use today are not as friendly, intuitive, and easy to use as we would want them to be. Sure, technology has gone a long way past typing obscure commands in a terminal to run a computer program or pressing seemingly arbitrary buttons in a confusing sequence to program a VCR. But, despite colorful displays, touch-sensitive interfaces, voice-activated assistants, and smarter artificial intelligence under the hood, we still have numerous problems that are far from being completely solved, from websites that misbehave depending on the browser you are using, to apps whose interfaces and layout change dramatically between one version and the next—an update that might have happened silently and without an easy option to "revert back to the version that made sense to me".

Here is my advice: (1) Don't be afraid to explore! Clicking on a button here, exploring a set of options under a menu there, may bring new knowledge and open the door to learning opportunities. Arguably, this is one of the reasons why young children learn to use complex devices and apps so quickly. Maybe we should try to be a bit more like them... After all—if you keep your devices protected against malware and your data backed up (e.g., in a cloud-based service)—many mistakes can be undone and should have no major consequence. (2) Keep learning! One of the reasons the neighbor's 12-year-old kid knows so much about computers is because he invests a lot of time using them, which invariably leads to learning more about how they work and what to do when certain things go wrong. In addition to learning from knowledgeable friends and family members, check out if there are classes or tutoring sessions in the local college or public library, for example. (3) Ask for help whenever you need it. There are many people out there who spend a significant portion of their time sharing their knowledge with others, with the legitimate intention of helping their fellow humans. Remember that engineers and programmers are ultimately problem solvers: we derive great satisfaction from helping a person solve a problem by following a specific set of instructions in a meaningful sequence. The feeling is magnified if that solution is made available in a respectable public forum (e.g., Stack Exchange[3]) and used again and again by other people trying to solve the same problem.

---

[1] http://evernote.com/.

[2] http://getpocket.com/.

[3] http://stackexchange.com/.

3. Privacy, security, and anonymity

Yes, there are bad guys out there. Unwanted email (known as *spam*)—usually associated with scams and often trying to look legit to trick us into clicking on a link that we should not—will continue to be a problem in the foreseeable future. And so will ID theft, database breaches, email leaks, and many other cybersecurity incidents that every now and then make to the headlines of the major news sources. Protecting our privacy, keeping our assets secure, and preserving anonymity are difficult goals to attain with 100 % success rate.

On these matters, here are some useful recommendations[4]:

- Protect your computer against intruders and malware. Keep your anti-virus and firewall software up-to-date. Don't click on links whose source you cannot verify. Beware of obscure websites or too-good-to-be-true offers. Resist the temptation to download free contents of copyrighted materials; besides the ethical and legal implications of your actions, you may inadvertently open the door of your computer and personal data to malicious individuals and organizations.
- Choose your passwords wisely and store them properly. Avoid the most common passwords, such as the ones made famous by Carnegie Mellon University Professor Lorrie Faith Cranor's *security blanket* [1]. To check how good is your choice of password, try http://howsecureismypassword.net/. Consider using a password manager app, such as 1Password,[5] Dashlane,[6] or LastPass.[7]
- Beware of spam, phishing, and scams. Since these are ever-changing threats, consider subscribing to a newsletter (or equivalent) with latest news and updates on security threats and instructions (in plain English) on how to stay safe and protected. For example, the Security Team from the Office of Information Technology at Florida Atlantic University (FAU) maintains a site that works as a "central location to find resources, policies and guidelines that address IT security" (http://fau.edu/security/) and an associated newsletter/blog targeted at regular (i.e., non-technical) users (http://wordpress.fau.edu/security/).

6.2   Final Reflections

When asked about the impact of these tremendous technological advancements of the past few decades, which have happened so quickly and taken us by storm, I position myself as a cautious optimist. I am an optimist, not only because I have

---

[4]For browser-related recommendations, please refer to Chap. 2; for smartphone-centric advice, see Chap. 3.

[5]http://agilebits.com/onepassword.

[6]http://www.dashlane.com/.

[7]http://lastpass.com.

seen many lives impacted for the better thanks to some of the technologies, devices, and apps described in this book, but also because I have been on the technical side of several of these developments and can speak to the driving forces that make developers, scientists, and engineers overcome multiple challenges to develop products that they firmly and sincerely believe to have the potential to improve the quality of human life. These are, for the most part, highly-trained individuals that want to go beyond their mathematical, scientific, and programming expertise and convert those skills into tangible solutions to existing problems.

I am cautious, on the other hand, because I still want technology to serve me, and not the other way around. We are all witnesses of the dramatic changes that ubiquitous gadgets with colorful bright-lit screens have brought to our lives. Smartphones, social networks, video games, and apps—to name just a few culprits—have changed our habits as families, our social interactions, and even some of our rituals. This has been a rich field for serious analysis—better left to sociologists, anthropologists, and psychologists—as well as many humorous and insightful cartoons.

Yes, looking down at a small screen may bring us entertainment, information, directions to our destination, or the latest updates on a dear friend's life or career, but it might also alienate us to all that is happening right here, right now, in the real world. Maybe we should remind ourselves, as often as necessary, to also *look up*,[8] away from any screen, untethered from this powerful bondage to our favorite gadget, and direct our attention to what is happening around us and what makes us human.

Reference

1. Cranor LF (2013) Security blanket. http://lorrie.cranor.org/blog/2013/08/12/security-blanket/

---

[8]This final sentence was inspired by the poem/video "Look Up", by Gary Turk (http://garyturk.com/portfolio-item/lookup/). If you are not among the 55 million people who have already seen it on YouTube, don't miss it.

Printed in the United States
By Bookmasters